greatest ever
baking

p

This is a Parragon Publishing Book
This edition published in 2004

Parragon Publishing
Queen Street House
4 Queen Street
Bath BA1 1HE, UK

ISBN: 1-40543-286-1

Printed in Indonesia

Produced by The Bridgewater Book Company Ltd

NOTE

Cup measurements in this book are for American cups. This book also uses
imperial and metric measurements. Follow the same units of measurement
throughout; do not mix imperial and metric.
All spoon measurements are level: teaspoons are assumed to be 5 ml and
tablespoons are assumed to be 15 ml. Unless otherwise stated, milk is assumed
to be whole milk, eggs and individual vegetables such as potatoes are medium,
and pepper is freshly ground black pepper.

The nutritional information provided for each recipe is per serving or per
person. Optional ingredients, variations, or serving suggestions have not been
included in the calculations. The times given for each recipe are an
approximate guide only because the preparation times may differ according
to the techniques used by different people and the cooking times may vary as
a result of the type of oven used.

Recipes using raw or very lightly cooked eggs should be
avoided by infants, the elderly, pregnant women, convalescents, and anyone
suffering from an illness.

Contents

Introduction

It may be a daunting prospect to bake your own bread, pastries, cookies, and cakes instead of buying them ready-made at a foodstore, but once you have acquired the basic skills—and armed yourself with a few of the "tricks"—it becomes fun, versatile, and rewarding.

There are a few points that will make sure your baking session is successful, whatever type of recipe you have chosen. So, before you start:

- Read through the recipe carefully, and make sure you have the right ingredients—using all-purpose flour when self-rising flour is specified, for example, may not produce the result you were expecting!
- Remember to preheat the oven to the right temperature.
- Make sure you are using the correct size and shape of pan or dish because the quantities given in the recipe are for the size of the pan specified.
- Prepare the cookware before you start assembling the ingredients—grease or line pans, dishes, or cookie sheets as directed in the recipe.
- Measure the ingredients accurately, and do any basic preparation, such as chopping, slicing, or grating, before you start cooking.
- Once you start cooking, follow the recipe step-by-step, in the order given. Using high-quality ingredients will give the best results—unbleached flours and unrefined sugars are available for baking; fresh vegetables, fish, and good-quality meat from a reliable supplier, and a good, extra-virgin olive oil will make all the difference to savory bakes.

Pie Dough
- Use metal pans, rather than porcelain dishes, for tarts.
- Use fat at room temperature, cut into small pieces.
- Use ice water for mixing.
- Pie dough benefits from cool ingredients and cold hands.
- Strain dry ingredients into a mixing bowl to incorporate air.
- Wrap dough in foil or plastic wrap and allow it to "rest" in the refrigerator for 30 minutes before using.

Bread
- Plan ahead—most bread recipes include one or two periods of "proving" (leaving the dough in a warm place to double its bulk).
- If the flour feels cool, warm it gently in an oven at a low temperature before using.
- Make sure the liquid is lukewarm, to activate the yeast.
- To knead dough, stretch it away from you with one hand, while pulling it toward you with the other, then fold in the edges, turn it around slightly, and repeat.
- To test whether bread is cooked, tap the base of the loaf—it should sound hollow if it is ready.

Cakes
- Using a loose-based pan will make it easier to turn out the cake.
- Bring all the ingredients to room temperature before starting to bake.
- If possible, use a hand-held electric mixer for "creaming" (beating together the butter and sugar until the mixture has a pourable consistency).
- Fold in dry ingredients very gently, using a metal spoon or spatula in a figure-eight movement. This lets the air get to the mixture and stops the cake becoming too heavy.
- When the cake is cooked, it should feel springy when pressed lightly. Alternatively, when a fine metal skewer is inserted into the center of the cake, it should come out clean if the cake is cooked.

Basic Recipes

Ragù Sauce

MAKES ABOUT 2½ CUPS

3 tbsp olive oil

3 tbsp butter

2 large onions, chopped

4 celery stalks, sliced thinly

1 cup chopped bacon

2 garlic cloves, chopped

4½ cups ground beef

2 tbsp tomato paste

1 tbsp all-purpose flour

14 oz/400 g canned chopped tomatoes

⅔ cup beef bouillon

⅔ cup red wine

2 tsp dried oregano

½ tsp freshly grated nutmeg

salt and pepper

1 Heat the oil and butter in a pan over medium heat. Add the onions, celery, and bacon and cook for 5 minutes, stirring constantly.

2 Stir in the garlic and ground beef and cook, stirring frequently, until the meat has lost its redness. Lower the heat and simmer for 10 minutes, stirring occasionally.

3 Increase the heat to medium, stir in the tomato paste and the flour, and cook for 1–2 minutes. Add the tomatoes, bouillon, and wine and bring to the boil, stirring constantly. Season to taste, then stir in the oregano and nutmeg. Lower the heat, then cover, and simmer for 45 minutes, stirring occasionally. The sauce is now ready to use.

Basic Pizza Dough

MAKES ONE 10-INCH/25-CM PIZZA

1½ cups all-purpose flour, plus extra for dusting

1 tsp salt

1 tsp active dry yeast

6 tbsp lukewarm water

1 tbsp olive oil

1 Strain the flour and salt into a large bowl and add the yeast. Pour in the water and oil and bring together to form a dough. Knead for 5 minutes, then leave in a warm place to rise until doubled in size.

2 Punch the air out from the dough, then knead lightly. Roll it out on a lightly floured counter, ready for use.

Fresh Vegetable Bouillon

This can be kept chilled for up to three days or frozen for up to three months. Salt is not added when cooking the stock: it is better to season it according to the dish in which it its to be used.

MAKES ABOUT 6¼ CUPS

9 oz/250 g shallots

1 large carrot, diced

1 celery stalk, chopped

½ fennel bulb

1 garlic clove

1 bay leaf

a few fresh parsley and
   tarragon sprigs

8 cups water

pepper

1 Place all the ingredients in a large pan and bring to a boil.

2 Skim off the surface scum with a flat spoon and reduce to a gentle simmer. Partially cover and cook for 45 minutes. Let cool.

3 Line a strainer with clean cheesecloth and place over a large pitcher or bowl. Pour the bouillon through the strainer, then discard the herbs and vegetables.

4 Cover and store in small quantities in the refrigerator for up to three days.

Pesto Sauce

MAKES ABOUT 1¼ CUPS

2 cups finely chopped fresh parsley

2 garlic cloves, crushed

½ cup pine nuts, crushed

2 tbsp chopped fresh basil leaves

⅔ cup freshly grated Parmesan cheese

⅔ cup olive oil

white pepper

1 Place all the ingredients in a food processor and process for 2 minutes. Alternatively, you can blend by hand using a pestle and mortar.

2 Season with white pepper, then transfer to a pitcher, cover with plastic wrap, and store in the refrigerator before using.

Desserts

Confirmed dessert lovers feel a meal is lacking if there isn't a tempting dessert to finish off the menu. Yet it is often possible to combine indulgence with healthy ingredients. A lot of the recipes in this chapter contain fruit, which is the perfect ingredient for healthy desserts that are still deliciously tempting, such as Hot Blackberry Sponge, Raspberry Shortcake, Paper-thin Fruit Pies, Apple Tart Tatin, and Baked Bananas. Some desserts are also packed full of protein-rich nuts, such as Pine Nut Tart and Almond Cheesecakes.

queen of desserts

serves eight

2 tbsp butter, plus extra for greasing

2½ cups milk

1¼ cups superfine sugar

finely grated rind of 1 orange

4 eggs, separated

1⅔ cups fresh bread crumbs

pinch of salt

6 tbsp orange marmalade

COOK'S TIP

If you prefer a crisper meringue, bake the dessert in the oven for an extra 5 minutes.

VARIATION

Substitute the same quantity of fine sponge cake crumbs for the bread crumbs and use raspberry, strawberry, or apricot preserve instead of orange marmalade

1 Grease a 6-cup/1.5-litre ovenproof dish with a little butter.

2 To make the custard, heat the milk in a pan with the butter, ¼ cup of the superfine sugar, and the grated orange rind, until just warm.

3 Whisk the egg yolks in a bowl. Gradually pour the warm milk over the eggs, stirring constantly.

4 Stir the bread crumbs into the pan, then transfer the mixture to the prepared dish, and let stand for about 15 minutes.

5 Bake in a preheated oven, 350°F/180°C, for 20–25 minutes, until the custard has just set. Remove the dish from the oven, but do not turn the oven off.

6 To make the meringue, whisk the egg whites with the salt until they stand in soft peaks. Whisk in the remaining sugar, a little at a time.

7 Spread the orange marmalade over the cooked custard. Top with the meringue, spreading it right to the edges of the dish.

8 Return to the oven and bake for another 20 minutes, until the meringue is crisp and golden.

bread & butter pudding

serves six

4 tbsp butter, softened

4–5 slices white or brown bread

4 tbsp chunky orange marmalade

grated rind of 1 lemon

½–¾ cup golden raisins

¼ cup chopped candied peel

1 tsp ground cinnamon or allspice

1 cooking apple, peeled, cored, and
    coarsely grated

scant ½ cup brown sugar

3 eggs

generous 2 cups milk

2 tbsp raw brown sugar

3 Add another layer of bread, cutting the slices so that they fit the dish.

4 Sprinkle over most of the remaining golden raisins and all the remaining candied peel, spice, and brown sugar, sprinkling it evenly over the bread. Top with a final layer of bread, again cutting to fit the dish.

5 Lightly beat the eggs and milk together in a large mixing bowl, then carefully strain the mixture over the bread in the ovenproof dish. If time allows, let the pudding stand for 20–30 minutes.

1 Use the softened butter to grease an ovenproof dish and to spread on 1 side of the slices of bread, then spread the bread evenly with the orange marmalade.

2 Place a layer of buttered bread in the base of the prepared dish and sprinkle with the grated lemon rind, half of the golden raisins, half of the candied peel, half of the cinnamon or allspice, all of the apple, and half of the brown sugar.

6 Sprinkle the top of the finished bread pudding with the raw brown sugar and sprinkle over the remaining golden raisins. Cook in a preheated oven , 400°F/200°C, for 50–60 minutes, until it has risen and turned golden brown. Serve hot, if you like, or let cool completely, then serve cold.

eve's dessert

serves six

6 tbsp butter, plus extra for greasing

1 lb/450 g cooking apples, peeled,
    cored, and sliced

1 tbsp lemon juice

⅓ cup granulated sugar

⅓ cup golden raisins

⅓ cup superfine sugar

1 egg, beaten

1¼ cups self-rising flour

3 tbsp milk

¼ cup sliced almonds

custard or heavy cream, to serve

COOK'S TIP

To increase the almond flavor,
add ¼ cup of ground almonds
with the flour in step 4.

1 Grease a 3½-cup/900-ml
ovenproof dish with a little butter.

2 Combine the sliced apples with
the lemon juice, granulated sugar,
and golden raisins. Spoon into the
greased dish.

3 Cream the butter and superfine
sugar together in a bowl until
pale. Add the egg, a little at a time.

4 Carefully fold in the self-rising
flour and stir in the milk to give
a pourable consistency.

5 Spread the mixture evenly over
the apples and sprinkle the top
with the sliced almonds.

6 Bake in a preheated oven,
350°F/180°C, for 40–45 minutes,
until the sponge topping has turned
golden brown.

7 Serve the dessert piping hot,
accompanied by homemade
custard or heavy cream.

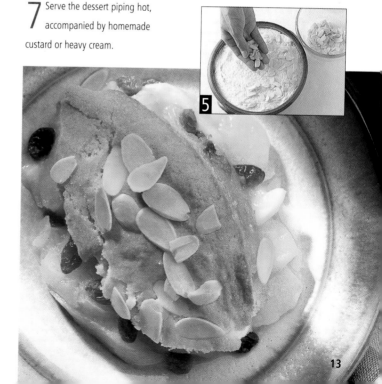

raspberry shortcake

serves eight

⅓ cup butter, diced, plus extra
    for greasing

1½ cups self-rising flour, plus extra
    for dusting

⅓ cup superfine sugar

1 egg yolk

1 tbsp rose water

2½ cups whipping cream,
    whipped lightly

1⅓ cups raspberries, plus extra
    for decoration

TO DECORATE

confectioners' sugar

fresh mint leaves (optional)

COOK'S TIP

The shortcake can be made a few
days in advance and stored in an
airtight container until required.

VARIATION

This shortcake is equally
delicious made with strawberries
or pitted and sliced peaches,
instead of raspberries.

1 Lightly grease 2 cookie sheets with a little butter.

2 To make the shortcake, strain the flour into a bowl.

3 Rub the butter into the flour with your fingertips until the mixture resembles bread crumbs.

4 Stir the sugar, egg yolk, and rose water into the mixture and bring together with your fingers to form a soft dough. Divide the dough in half.

5 Roll each piece of dough into an 8-inch/20-cm circle on a lightly floured counter. Carefully lift each one with the rolling pin onto a prepared cookie sheet, then crimp the edges of the dough.

6 Bake in a preheated oven, 375°F/190°C, for 15 minutes, until lightly golden. Transfer the shortcakes to a wire rack and let cool.

7 Mix the whipped cream with the raspberries and spoon on top of one of the shortcakes. Top with the other shortcake circle, dust with a little confectioners' sugar, and decorate with the extra raspberries and mint leaves, if you like.

plum cobbler

serves six

6 tbsp butter, melted and cooled,
plus extra for greasing

2 lb 4 oz/1 kg plums, pitted
and sliced

½ cup superfine sugar

1 tbsp lemon juice

2¼ cups all-purpose flour

⅓ cup granulated sugar

2 tsp baking powder

1 egg, beaten

⅔ cup buttermilk

heavy cream, to serve

1 Lightly grease an 8-cup/2-litre ovenproof dish with a little butter.

2 Combine the sliced plums, superfine sugar, lemon juice, and ¼ cup of the all-purpose flour in a large bowl.

3 Spoon the coated plums into the base of the prepared ovenproof dish, spreading them out evenly.

4 Strain the remaining flour and baking powder into a bowl. Stir in the granulated sugar.

5 Add the beaten egg, buttermilk, and cooled melted butter. Mix everything gently together to form a soft dough.

6 Place spoonfuls of the dough on top of the fruit mixture until it is almost completely covered.

7 Bake in a preheated oven, 375°F/190°C, for 35–40 minutes, until the dough is golden brown and the fruit mixture is bubbling.

8 Serve the cobbler piping hot, with heavy cream.

hot blackberry sponge

serves four

6 tbsp butter, melted, plus extra
   for greasing

1 lb/450 g blackberries

⅓ cup superfine sugar

1 egg

⅓ cup brown sugar, plus extra
   for sprinkling

½ cup milk

scant 1 cup self-rising flour

1 Lightly grease a 3½-cup/900-ml
ovenproof dish with a little butter.

2 Gently combine the blackberries
and superfine sugar in a large
mixing bowl until well blended.

3 Transfer the blackberry and sugar
mixture to the prepared dish,
spreading it out evenly.

4 In a separate bowl, beat the egg
and brown sugar together. Stir in
the melted butter and milk.

VARIATION

You can add 2 tablespoons of
cocoa powder to the batter in
step 5, if you like.

5 Strain the flour into the egg and
butter mixture and fold together
lightly, until the mixture forms a
smooth batter.

6 Carefully spread the batter over
the blackberry and sugar mixture
in the ovenproof dish.

7 Bake the sponge in a preheated
oven, 350°F/180°C, for about
25–30 minutes, until the topping is
firm and golden.

8 Sprinkle the sponge with a little
brown sugar and serve hot.

treacle tart

9 oz/250 g ready-made unsweetened
 pastry dough, thawed if frozen
1 cup light corn syrup
scant 2 cups fresh white
 bread crumbs
½ cup heavy cream
finely grated rind of ½ lemon
 or orange
2 tbsp lemon or orange juice
homemade custard, to serve

COOK'S TIP

Syrup is notoriously sticky and so
can be quite difficult to measure.
Dip the spoon in hot water first
and the syrup will slide off it
more easily and completely.

VARIATION

Use the dough trimmings to
create a lattice pattern on top of
the tart, if you wish.

---

1 Roll out the pie dough on a lightly
 floured counter and use it to line
an 8-inch/20-cm loose-based tart pan,
reserving the dough trimmings. Prick
the bottom of the tart shell with
a fork and chill in the refrigerator
for 30 minutes.

2 Cut out small shapes from the
 reserved dough trimmings, such
as leaves, stars, or hearts, to decorate
the top of the tart.

3 Combine the light corn syrup,
 bread crumbs, heavy cream,
grated lemon or orange rind, and
lemon or orange juice in a bowl.

4 Pour the mixture into the tart shell
 and decorate the edges of the tart
with the dough cut-outs.

5 Bake in a preheated oven,
 375°F/190°C, for 35–40 minutes,
or until the filling is just set.

6 Let the tart cool slightly in the pan
 Turn out and serve hot or cold
with homemade custard.

apple tart tatin

serves eight

generous ½ cup butter

scant ⅔ cup superfine sugar

4 eating apples, cored and cut
    into fourths

9 oz/250 g ready-made unsweetened
    pastry dough, thawed if frozen

crème fraîche, to serve

1 Heat the butter and sugar in a 9-inch/23-cm ovenproof skillet over medium heat for about 5 minutes, until the mixture starts to caramelize. Remove the skillet from the heat.

2 Arrange the apple fourths, skin side down, in the skillet, taking care as the butter and sugar will be very hot. Place the skillet back on the heat and simmer for 2 minutes.

3 Roll out the dough on a lightly floured counter to form a circle just a little larger than the skillet.

4 Place the dough over the apples, press down, and carefully tuck in the edges to seal the apples underneath the layer of dough.

5 Bake in a preheated oven, 400°F/200°C, for 20–25 minutes, until the dough is golden. Remove from the oven and cool for about 10 minutes.

6 Place a serving plate over the skillet and invert so that the dough forms the base of the turned-out tart. Serve with crème fraîche.

fruit crumble tart

DOUGH

1¼ cups all-purpose flour, plus extra
   for dusting

2 tbsp superfine sugar

½ cup butter, diced

1 tbsp water

FILLING

1½ cups raspberries

1 lb/450 g plums, halved, pitted,
   and coarsely chopped

3 tbsp raw brown sugar

TOPPING

scant 1 cup all-purpose flour

⅓ cup raw brown sugar

⅓ cup butter, diced

⅔ cup chopped mixed nuts

1 tsp ground cinnamon

light cream or ice cream,
   to serve

1 To make the dough, place the flour, sugar, and butter in a bowl and rub in the butter with your fingertips. Add the water and bring together with your fingers to form a soft dough. Wrap in plastic wrap and chill in the refrigerator for 30 minutes.

2 Roll out the dough on a lightly floured counter and use it to line the base of a 9½-inch/24-cm loose-based tart pan. Prick the base of the tart shell with a fork and chill in the refrigerator for about 30 minutes.

3 To make the filling, toss the raspberries and plums together with the sugar and spoon into the tart shell.

4 To make the crumble topping, combine the flour, sugar, and butter in a bowl. Rub in the butter with your fingertips until the mixture resembles coarse bread crumbs. Stir in the nuts and ground cinnamon.

5 Sprinkle the crumble topping over the fruit and press down gently with the back of a spoon. Bake in a preheated oven, 400°F/200°C, for 20–25 minutes, until the topping has turned golden brown. Serve the tart with light cream or ice cream.

paper-thin fruit pies

serves four

1 medium eating apple

1 medium ripe pear

2 tbsp lemon juice

4 tbsp lowfat margarine

4 sheets of phyllo pastry, thawed
    if frozen

2 tbsp low-sugar apricot preserve

1 tbsp unsweetened orange juice

1 tbsp finely chopped pistachios

2 tsp confectioners' sugar,
    for dusting

lowfat custard, to serve

COOK'S TIP

Keep the unused sheets of phyllo
pastry covered with a clean,
damp dish towel until you are
ready to use them, as they dry
out easily.

VARIATION

Other combinations of fruit are
equally delicious. Try peach and
apricot, raspberry, and apple, or
pineapple and mango.

1 Core and thinly slice the apple
and pear and toss them in the
lemon juice.

2 Gently melt the lowfat spread in a
small pan over low heat. Cut each
sheet of phyllo pastry into 4 and cover
with a clean, damp dish towel. Brush
4 large nonstick muffin pans,
10 cm/4 inches wide, with a little
of the lowfat spread.

3 Working on each pie separately,
brush 4 sheets of pastry with
lowfat spread. Press a small sheet
of pastry into the base of one pan.
Arrange the other sheets on top at
slightly different angles. Repeat with
the other sheets to make another
3 pies.

4 Arrange the apple and pear slices
alternately in the center of each
phyllo pastry case and lightly crimp the
edges of the pastry of each pie.

5 Combine the preserve and orange
juice until smooth and brush over
the fruit. Bake in a preheated oven,
400°F/200°C, for 12–15 minutes.

6 Sprinkle with the chopped
pistachios, dust lightly with
confectioners' sugar, and serve hot
with lowfat custard.

custard tart

serves eight

DOUGH

1¼ cups all-purpose flour, plus extra
for dusting

2 tbsp superfine sugar

½ cup butter, diced

1 tbsp water

FILLING

3 eggs

⅔ cup light cream

⅔ cup milk

freshly grated nutmeg

1 To make the dough, place the flour and sugar in a bowl and rub in the butter with your fingertips until the mixture resembles bread crumbs.

2 Add the water and bring together with your fingers to form a soft dough. Wrap in plastic wrap and chill in the refrigerator for 30 minutes.

3 Roll out the dough to a circle on a lightly floured counter and use to line a 9½-inch/24-cm loose-based tart pan.

4 Trim the edges of the tart shell. Prick the base with a fork and chill in the refrigerator for 30 minutes.

5 Line the tart shell with foil and baking beans.

6 Bake in a preheated oven, at 375°F/190°C, for 15 minutes. Remove the foil and beans and bake for a further 15 minutes.

7 To make the filling, whisk the eggs, cream, milk, and nutmeg together. Pour the filling into the prepared tart shell. Return the tart to the oven and cook for 25–30 minutes, or until the filling is just set, then serve.

baked sweet ravioli

SWEET PASTA DOUGH

3¾ cups all-purpose flour, plus extra
   for dusting

⅔ cup butter, plus extra
   for greasing

¾ cup superfine sugar

4 eggs

1 oz/25 g yeast

½ cup lukewarm milk

FILLING

⅔ cup chestnut paste

½ cup unsweetened cocoa

generous ¼ cup superfine sugar

½ cup chopped almonds

1 cup crushed amaretti cookies

generous ½ cup orange marmalade

1 To make the sweet pasta dough, strain the flour into a large mixing bowl, then mix in the butter, sugar, and 3 of the eggs.

2 Combine the yeast and lukewarm milk in a small bowl and when thoroughly blended, mix into the dough.

3 Knead the dough for 20 minutes, then cover with a clean cloth, and let stand in a warm place for 1 hour to rise.

4 In a separate bowl, combine the chestnut paste, unsweetened cocoa, sugar, almonds, crushed amaretti cookies, and orange marmalade until blended.

5 Grease 1 or 2 cookie sheets with a little butter.

6 Roll out the pasta dough into a thin sheet on a lightly floured counter, and cut into 2-inch/5-cm circles with a plain cookie cutter.

7 Put a spoonful of filling onto each circle, then fold in half, pressing the edges firmly together to seal. Arrange the ravioli on the prepared cookie sheet, spacing them out well.

8 Beat the remaining egg and brush over the ravioli to glaze. Bake in a preheated oven, 350°F/180°C, for 20 minutes. Serve hot.

lemon tart

serves eight

DOUGH

1¼ cups all-purpose flour, plus extra
   for dusting

2 tbsp superfine sugar

½ cup butter, diced

1 tbsp water

FILLING

⅔ cup heavy cream

½ cup superfine sugar

4 eggs

grated rind of 3 lemons

¾ cup lemon juice

confectioners' sugar, for dusting

COOK'S TIP

To avoid any spillage, pour half
of the filling into the tart **shell**,
place in the oven, **then pour in**
the remaining filling.

---

1 To make the dough, place the
flour and sugar in a bowl and rub
in the butter with your fingertips until
the mixture resembles bread crumbs.
Add the water and bring together to
form a dough. Wrap in plastic wrap
and chill for 30 minutes.

2 Roll out the dough on a lightly
floured counter and use it to line
a 9½-inch/24-cm loose-based tart pan.
Prick the base of the tart shell with a
fork and chill in the refrigerator for
30 minutes.

3 Line the tart shell with foil and
baking beans and bake in a
preheated oven, 375°F/190°C, for
15 minutes. Remove the foil and
baking beans and cook the tart shell
for 15 minutes more.

4 To make the filling, whisk the
cream, sugar, eggs, lemon rind,
and juice together until thoroughly
blended. Place the tart shell, still in its
pan, on a cookie sheet, and pour in the
filling (see Cook's Tip).

5 Bake the tart in the preheated
oven for about 20 minutes, or
until the filling is just set. Let cool, then
lightly dust with confectioners' sugar,
and serve.

pine nut tart

serves eight

DOUGH

1¼ cups all-purpose flour, plus extra
     for dusting

2 tbsp superfine sugar

½ cup butter, diced

1 tbsp water

FILLING

1½ cups farmer's cheese

4 tbsp heavy cream

3 eggs

½ cup superfine sugar

grated rind of 1 orange

1 cup pine nuts

1 To make the dough, place the flour and sugar in a bowl and rub in the butter with your fingertips until the mixture resembles bread crumbs. Add the water and bring the mixture together with your fingers to form a soft dough. Wrap in plastic wrap and chill in the refrigerator for 30 minutes.

2 Roll out the dough on a lightly floured counter and use it to line a 9½-inch/24-cm loose-based tart pan. Prick the base of the tart shell with a fork and chill for 30 minutes.

3 Line the tart shell with foil and baking beans and bake in a preheated oven,t 375°F/190°C, for 15 minutes. Remove the foil and baking beans and cook the shell for 15 minutes more.

4 To make the filling, beat the farmer's cheese, cream, eggs, sugar, orange rind, and half of the pine nuts together in a bowl. Pour the filling into the tart shell and sprinkle with the remaining pine nuts.

5 Reduce the oven to 325°F/160°C and bake the tart for about 35 minutes, or until the filling is just set. Let cool before removing from the pan and serving.

VARIATION

Replace the pine nuts with sliced almonds, if you like.

orange tart

serves six—eight

DOUGH

1¼ cups all-purpose flour, plus extra
for dusting

2 tbsp superfine sugar

½ cup butter, diced

1 tbsp water

FILLING

grated rind of 2 oranges

scant ⅔ cup orange juice

scant 1 cup fresh white
bread crumbs

2 tbsp lemon juice

⅔ cup light cream

4 tbsp butter

¼ cup superfine sugar

2 eggs, separated

salt

TO SERVE

whipped cream

grated orange rind

1 To make the dough, place the
flour and sugar in a bowl and rub
in the butter with your fingertips until
the mixture resembles bread crumbs.
Add the water and bring the mixture
together with your fingers to form a
soft dough. Wrap in plastic wrap and
chill in the refrigerator for 30 minutes.

2 Roll out the dough on a lightly
floured counter and use it to line
a 9½-inch/24-cm loose-based tart pan.
Prick the base of the tart shell with a
fork and chill in the refrigerator for
30 minutes.

3 Line the tart shell with foil and
baking beans and bake in a
preheated oven, 375°F/190°C, for
15 minutes. Remove the foil and beans
and cook for 15 minutes more.

4 To make the filling, combine the
orange rind and juice with the
bread crumbs together in a bowl. Stir
in the lemon juice and light cream.
Melt the butter and sugar in a small

pan over low heat. Remove the pan
from the heat, add the 2 egg yolks, a
pinch of salt, and the bread crumb
mixture, and stir.

5 Whisk the egg whites with a
pinch of salt in a mixing bowl
until they form soft peaks. Fold them
into the egg yolk mixture.

6 Pour the filling mixture into the
tart shell. Bake in a preheated
oven, 325°F/160°C, for about
45 minutes, or until just set. Let cool
slightly and serve warm.

coconut cream tart

serves six—eight

DOUGH

1¼ cups all-purpose flour, plus extra
   for dusting

2 tbsp superfine sugar

½ cup butter, diced

1 tbsp water

FILLING

scant 2 cups milk

generous ½ cup coconut cream

3 egg yolks

½ cup superfine sugar

generous ⅓ cup all-purpose
   flour, sifted

¼ cup dry unsweetened coconut,
   plus extra to decorate

generous ¼ cup chopped candied
   pineapple, plus extra to decorate

2 tbsp rum or pineapple juice

1⅓ cups whipping cream, whipped

1 To make the dough, place the flour and sugar in a bowl and rub in the butter with your fingertips until the mixture resembles bread crumbs. Add the water and bring the mixture together with your fingers to form a soft dough. Wrap in plastic wrap and chill in the refrigerator for 30 minutes.

2 Roll out the dough on a lightly floured counter and use it to line a 9½-inch/24-cm loose-based tart pan. Prick the base of the tart shell with a fork and chill in the refrigerator for 30 minutes.

3 Line the tart shell with foil and baking beans and bake in a preheated oven, 375°F/190°C, for 15 minutes. Remove the foil and baking beans and cook for 15 minutes more. Let cool.

4 To make the filling, pour the milk into a small pan and add the coconut cream. Set over a low heat and bring to just below boiling point, stirring constantly until the mixture is thickened and smooth.

5 Whisk the egg yolks and the sugar together in a bowl until pale and fluffy. Whisk in the flour. Pour the hot milk over the egg mixture, stirring constantly. Return to the pan and heat gently, stirring constantly, for about 8 minutes, until thick. Let cool.

6 Stir in the coconut, pineapple, and rum or juice. Spread in the tart. Cover with cream and decorate with candied pineapple and coconut.

apricot & cranberry tart

serves eight

DOUGH
1¼ cups all-purpose flour, plus extra
   for dusting
2 tbsp superfine sugar
½ cup butter, diced
1 tbsp water

FILLING
scant 1 cup sweet butter
1 cup superfine sugar
1 egg
2 egg yolks
⅓ cup all-purpose flour, sifted
1⅔ cups ground almonds
4 tbsp heavy cream
14½ oz/410 g canned apricot
   halves, drained
generous 1 cup fresh cranberries

1 To make the dough, place the flour and sugar in a bowl and rub in the butter with your fingertips until the mixture resembles bread crumbs. Add the water and bring the mixture together with your fingers to form a soft dough. Wrap in plastic wrap and chill in the refrigerator for 30 minutes.

2 Roll out the dough on a lightly floured counter and use it to line a 9½-inch/24-cm loose-based tart pan. Prick the base of the tart shell with a fork and chill in the refrigerator for 30 minutes.

3 Line the tart shell with foil and baking beans and bake in a preheated oven, 375°F/190°C, for

15 minutes. Remove the foil and baking beans and cook the tart shell for 10 minutes more.

4 To make the filling, cream the butter and sugar together in a bowl until light and fluffy. Beat in the egg and egg yolks, then stir in the flour, almonds, and cream.

5 Place the apricot halves and cranberries on the base of the tart shell and spoon the filling mixture over the top.

6 Bake in the preheated oven for about 1 hour, or until the topping is just set. Let cool slightly, then serve warm or cold.

cheese & apple tart

serves eight

1 tbsp butter, for greasing

1½ cups self-rising flour

1 tsp baking powder

pinch of salt

⅓ cup brown sugar

generous 1 cup pitted
  dates, chopped

1 lb 2 oz/500 g eating apples, cored
  and chopped

¼ cup chopped walnuts

¼ cup sunflower oil

2 eggs

1¾ cups grated colby cheese

COOK'S TIP

This is a deliciously moist
tart. Any leftovers should be
stored in the refrigerator and
heated through before serving.

1 Grease a 9½-inch/23-cm loose-
based tart pan with the butter
and line with baking parchment.

2 Strain the flour, baking powder,
and salt into a large bowl. Stir in
the brown sugar and the chopped
dates, apples, and walnuts. Mix
together until thoroughly blended.

3 Beat the oil and eggs together
and add the mixture to the dry
ingredients. Stir with a wooden spoon
until well blended.

4 Spoon half of the mixture into
the prepared pan and level the
surface with the back of a spoon.

5 Sprinkle with the grated cheese,
then spoon over the remaining
cake mix, spreading it to the edges
of the pan.

6 Bake in a preheated oven, 350°F/
180°C, for 45–50 minutes, or
until golden and firm to the touch.

7 Let the tart cool slightly in the
pan, then turn out of the pan,
and serve warm.

2

3

5

mincemeat & grape jalousie

serves four

1 tbsp butter, for greasing

1lb 2 oz/500 g ready-made puff
pastry dough, thawed if frozen

14½ oz/410 g jar sweet mincemeat

1 cup grapes, seeded and cut
in half

1 egg, beaten lightly

raw brown sugar, for sprinkling

COOK'S TIP

Puff pastry has a high proportion
of fat—this is what gives it its
characteristic layered appearance
and light, crisp texture. However,
this also makes it more fragile
than other types of pastry, so
handle it as lightly and as
little as possible.

VARIATION

For an enhanced festive flavor,
stir 2 tablespoons of sherry into
the mincemeat

1 Lightly grease a cookie sheet
with the butter.

2 Roll out the puff pie dough on a
lightly floured counter and cut
into 2 rectangles.

3 Place one dough rectangle on the
prepared cookie sheet and brush
the edges with water.

4 Combine the mincemeat and
grapes in a mixing bowl. Spread
the mixture evenly over the dough
rectangle on the cookie sheet, leaving
a 1-inch/2.5-cm border.

5 Fold the second pie dough
rectangle in half lengthwise,
and cut a series of parallel lines across
the folded edge with a sharp knife,
leaving a 1-inch/2.5-cm border.

6 Open out the second rectangle
and lay it over the mincemeat
filling. Press the edges of the pie
dough together to seal.

7 Flute and crimp the edges of the
dough with your fingers. Lightly
brush with the beaten egg to glaze
and sprinkle with raw brown sugar.

8 Bake in a preheated oven,
425°F/220°C, for 15 minutes.
Reduce the heat to 350°F/180°C and
cook for 30 minutes more, until the
jalousie is well risen and golden brown.

9 Transfer to a wire rack to cool
completely before serving.

lime frangipane tartlets

makes twelve

scant 1 cup all-purpose flour, plus
    extra for dusting

⅓ cup butter, softened

1 tsp grated lime rind

1 tbsp lime juice

¼ cup superfine sugar

1 egg

¼ cup ground almonds

⅓ cup confectioners' sugar, sifted

½ tbsp water

1 Reserve 5 teaspoons of the flour and 3 teaspoons of the butter and set aside until required.

2 Rub the remaining butter into the remaining flour with your fingertips until the mixture resembles fine bread crumbs. Stir in the lime rind, followed by the lime juice, then bring the mixture together with your fingers to form a soft dough.

3 Roll out the dough thinly on a lightly floured counter. Stamp out 12 circles, 3-inches/7.5-cm wide, and line a shallow muffin pan.

4 Cream the reserved butter and superfine sugar together in a bowl until pale and fluffy.

5 Mix in the egg, then the ground almonds and the reserved flour.

6 Divide the mixture among the tartlet shells and smooth the tops.

7 Bake in a preheated oven, 400°F/200°C, for 15 minutes, until set and lightly golden. Turn out onto a wire rack to cool.

8 Mix the confectioners' sugar with the water. Drizzle a little of the frosting over each tartlet and serve.

pear tarts

serves six

9 oz/250 g ready-made puff pie
    dough, thawed if frozen
2 tbsp brown sugar
2 tbsp butter, plus extra for brushing
1 tbsp finely chopped
    preserved ginger
3 pears, peeled, cored, and halved
cream, to serve

COOK'S TIP

If you like, serve these tarts
with vanilla ice cream for a
delicious dessert.

1 Roll out the dough on a lightly floured counter. Stamp out 6 x circles, about 4 inches/10 cm wide.

2 Place the circles on a large cookie sheet and chill in the refrigerator for 30 minutes.

3 Cream the brown sugar and butter together in a small bowl, then stir in the preserved ginger.

4 Prick the dough with a fork, then spread with the ginger mixture.

5 Slice the pear halves lengthwise, keeping them intact at the tip. Fan out the slices slightly.

6 Place a fanned-out pear half on top of each dough circle. Make small flutes around the edges of the circles. Brush the pears with butter.

7 Bake in a preheated oven, 400°F/200°C, for 15–20 minutes, until the pastry is well risen and golden. Let the tarts cool slightly before serving warm with a little cream.

crème brûlée tarts

DOUGH

1¼ cups all-purpose flour, plus extra
   for dusting

2 tbsp superfine sugar

½ cup butter, diced

1 tbsp water

FILLING

4 egg yolks

¼ cup superfine sugar

1¾ cups heavy cream

1 tsp vanilla extract

raw brown sugar, for sprinkling

1 To make the dough, place the flour and sugar in a bowl and rub in the butter with your fingertips until the mixture resembles bread crumbs. Add the water and bring the mixture together with your fingers to form a soft dough. Wrap in plastic wrap and chill in the refrigerator for 30 minutes.

2 Divide the dough into 6 pieces. Roll out the dough on a lightly floured counter and use it to line 6 tartlet pans, 4 inches/10 cm wide. Prick the base of the dough with a fork and chill in the refrigerator for 20 minutes.

3 Line the tart shells with foil and baking beans and bake in a preheated oven, 375°F/190°C, for 15 minutes. Remove the foil and beans and cook for 10 minutes more, until crisp and golden. Let cool.

4 Meanwhile, make the filling. Beat the egg yolks and sugar together in a bowl until pale. Heat the cream and vanilla extract in a pan until just below boiling point, then pour onto the egg mixture, whisking constantly.

5 Return the mixture to a clean pan and bring to just below a boil, stirring constantly until thick. Do not let the mixture boil or it will curdle.

6 Let the mixture cool slightly, then pour into the tart shells. Let cool, then chill in the refrigerator overnight.

7 Sprinkle the tarts with brown sugar. Place under a preheated hot broiler for a few minutes. Let cool, then chill for 2 hours before serving.

pavlova

1 Line a cookie sheet with a sheet of baking parchment. Whisk the egg whites with the salt in a large bowl until they form soft peaks.

2 Whisk in the superfine sugar, a little at a time, whisking well after each addition until all of the sugar has been incorporated and the meringue is smooth and glossy.

3 Spoon three-fourths of the meringue onto the cookie sheet, forming an 8-inch/20-cm circle.

4 Place spoonfuls of the remaining meringue all around the edge of the circle to join up to make a neat nest shape.

5 Bake in a preheated oven, 275°F/140°C, for 1¼ hours.

6 Turn the heat off, but leave the pavlova in the oven until it is completely cold.

7 Place the pavlova on a serving dish. Spread with the lightly whipped cream, then arrange the fresh fruit on top. Do not add the cream and fruit too far in advance, or the pavlova will go soggy.

almond cheesecakes

serves four

12 amaretti cookies

1 egg white, beaten lightly

1 cup skim-milk soft cheese

½ tsp almond extract

½ tsp finely grated lime rind

scant ¼ cup ground almonds

2 tbsp superfine sugar

⅓ cup golden raisins

2 tsp powdered gelatin

2 tbsp boiling water

2 tbsp lime juice

TO DECORATE

2 tbsp toasted sliced almonds

strips of lime rind

1 Place the cookies in a plastic bag, seal the bag, and using a rolling pin, crush them into small pieces.

2 Place the amaretti crumbs in a bowl and stir in the egg white to bind them together.

3 Line a cookie sheet with baking parchment or use a nonstick tray. Arrange 4 nonstick pastry rings or poached egg rings, 3½ inches/9 cm wide, on top. Divide the amaretti mixture into 4 equal portions and spoon it into the rings, pressing it down well. Bake in a preheated oven, 350°F/180°C, for about 10 minutes, until crisp. Remove from the oven and let cool in the rings.

4 Place the soft cheese, almond extract, lime rind, ground almonds, sugar, and golden raisins in a bowl and beat thoroughly until well blended.

5 Dissolve the gelatin in the boiling water and stir in the lime juice. Fold into the cheese mixture and spoon over the amaretti bases. Smooth over the tops and chill in the refrigerator for 1 hour, or until set.

6 Loosen the cheesecakes from the rings using a small spatula and transfer to serving plates. Decorate with toasted sliced almonds and strips of lime rind and serve.

baked bananas

serves four

4 bananas

2 passion fruit

4 tbsp orange juice

4 tbsp orange-flavored liqueur

ORANGE-FLAVORED CREAM

⅔ cup heavy cream

3 tbsp confectioners' sugar

2 tbsp orange-flavored liqueur

VARIATION

Leave the bananas in their skins for a really quick dessert. Split the banana skins and pop in 1–2 squares of chocolate. Wrap the bananas in foil and bake for 10 minutes, or until the chocolate just melts.

---

1 To make the orange-flavored cream, pour the heavy cream into a mixing bowl and sprinkle over the confectioners' sugar. Whisk the mixture until it is standing in soft peaks. Carefully fold in the orange-flavored liqueur and chill in the refrigerator until required.

2 Peel the bananas and place each one on a sheet of foil.

3 Cut the passion fruit in half and squeeze the juice of each half over each banana. Spoon orange juice and liqueur over each banana.

4 Fold the foil sheets over the top of the bananas, tucking the ends in so they are completely enclosed.

5 Place the parcels on a cookie sheet and bake the bananas in a preheated oven, 350°F/180°C, for about 10 minutes, or until they are just tender (test by inserting a toothpick).

6 Transfer the foil parcels to warmed serving plates. Open out the banana parcels at the table, then serve immediately with the chilled orange-flavored cream.

baked apples with berries

serves four

4 medium cooking apples

1 tbsp lemon juice

1 cup prepared blackberries,
  thawed if frozen

1 tbsp sliced almonds

½ tsp ground allspice

½ tsp finely grated lemon rind

2 tbsp raw brown sugar

1¼ cups ruby port

1 cinnamon stick, broken

2 tsp cornstarch blended with
  2 tbsp cold water

lowfat custard, to serve

1 Wash and dry the apples. Make a shallow cut through the skin around the middle of each apple using a small sharp knife—this will help the apples to cook through.

2 Core the apples, brush the centers with the lemon juice to prevent them from discoloring, then stand them in an ovenproof dish.

3 Mix the blackberries, almonds, allspice, lemon rind, and sugar in a bowl Spoon the mixture into the center of each apple with a teaspoon.

4 Pour the port into the dish, add the cinnamon stick, and bake the apples in a preheated oven, 400°F/200°C, for 35–40 minutes, or until tender and soft.

5 Drain the cooking juices into a small pan. Keep the apples warm.

6 Remove the cinnamon and discard, then add the cornstarch mixture to the pan. Cook over medium heat, stirring constantly, until the mixture has thickened.

7 Heat the lowfat custard until piping hot. Pour the sauce over the apples and serve with the custard.

44

baked pears with cinnamon

serves four

4 ripe pears

2 tbsp lemon juice

¼ cup light brown sugar

1 tsp ground cinnamon

5 tbsp lowfat spread

finely grated lemon rind, to decorate

lowfat custard, to serve

1 Core and peel the pears, then slice them in half lengthwise, and brush all over with the lemon juice to prevent them from discoloring. Arrange the pear halves, cored sides down, in a small nonstick roasting pan.

2 Place the sugar, cinnamon, and lowfat spread in a small pan over low heat, stirring constantly, until the sugar has completely dissolved. Keep the heat as low as possible to prevent too much water evaporating from the lowfat spread as it starts to get hot. Spoon the sugar mixture over the pears.

3 Bake in a preheated oven, 400°F/200°C, for 20–25 minutes, or until the pears are tender and golden, occasionally spooning the sugar mixture over the fruit during the cooking time.

4 To serve, heat the lowfat custard until it is piping hot and spoon a little onto 4 warmed dessert plates, then arrange 2 pear halves on each plate.

5 Decorate the pears with a little finely grated lemon rind and serve immediately.

italian bread pudding

serves four

1 tbsp butter, for greasing

2 small eating apples, peeled,
   cored, and sliced into rings

generous ⅓ cup granulated sugar

2 tbsp white wine

3½ oz/100 g bread, sliced with
   crusts removed (slightly stale
   French baguette is ideal)

1¼ cups light cream

2 eggs, beaten

pared rind of 1 orange, cut into
   thin sticks

VARIATION

For a change, try adding
some dried fruit, such as
apricots, cherries, or dates, to
the pudding, if you like.

1 Grease a 5-cup/1.2-litre deep
  ovenproof dish with the butter.

2 Arrange the apple rings across the
  base of the dish, overlapping
them, then sprinkle half of the sugar
over the apples.

3 Pour the wine over the apples.
  Add the bread slices, pushing
them down with your hands to flatten
them slightly.

4 Mix the cream with the eggs,
  the remaining sugar, and the
orange rind and pour the mixture
over the bread. Set aside to soak
for 30 minutes.

5 Bake the pudding in a preheated
  oven, 350°F/180,°C for about
25 minutes, until golden and set.
Remove from the oven and serve.

COOK'S TIP

Some varieties of eating apples
are better for cooking than
others. Among the most suitable
are Blenheim Orange, Cox's
Orange Pippin, Egremont Russet,
Granny Smith, Idared, James
Grieve, Jonagold, Jonathan
McIntosh, Northern Spy,
and Winesap.

tuscan delight

serves four

1 tbsp butter, for greasing

⅔ cup mixed dried fruit

generous 1 cup ricotta cheese

3 egg yolks

¼ cup superfine sugar

1 tsp ground cinnamon

finely grated rind of 1 orange, plus
    extra to decorate

crème fraîche, to serve (optional)

COOK'S TIP

Crème fraîche has a slightly sour, nutty taste and is very thick. It is suitable for cooking, but has the same fat content as heavy cream. It can be made by stirring cultured buttermilk into heavy cream and refrigerating it overnight.

1 Grease 4 mini ovenproof bowls or ramekin dishes with the butter.

2 Place the dried fruit in a bowl and cover with warm water. Set aside to soak for 10 minutes.

3 Beat the ricotta cheese with the egg yolks in a bowl. Stir in the superfine sugar, cinnamon, and orange rind and mix well.

4 Drain the soaked fruit in a strainer set over a bowl. Add the drained fruit to the ricotta cheese mixture and stir to blend.

5 Spoon the mixture into the prepared bowls or dishes.

6 Bake in a preheated oven, 350°F/ 180°C, for 15 minutes. The tops should just be firm to the touch, but should not have browned.

7 Decorate the desserts with grated orange rind. Serve warm or chilled with a spoonful of crème fraîche, if you like.

mascarpone cheesecake

serves eight

1½ tbsp sweet butter, plus extra
    for greasing

3 cups ginger cookie crumbs

1 tablespoon chopped
    preserved ginger

2¼ cups mascarpone cheese

finely grated rind and juice of 2 lemons

½ cup superfine sugar

2 extra large eggs, separated

fruit coulis (see Cook's Tip), to serve

COOK'S TIP

Fruit coulis can be made
by cooking 3½ cups
fruit, such as blueberries, for
5 minutes with 2 tablespoons of
water. Strain the mixture, then
stir in 1 tablespoon (or more to
taste) of strained confectioners'
sugar. Let cool before serving.

1 Grease the base of a 10-inch/
25-cm spring-form cake pan or
loose-based pan with butter and line
with baking parchment.

2 Melt the butter in a pan over
low heat and stir in the crushed
cookies and ginger. Use the mixture to
line the pan, pressing it about ¼ inch/
5 mm up the sides.

3 Beat the cheese, lemon rind and
juice, sugar, and egg yolks
together in a bowl until quite smooth.

4 Whisk the egg whites until stiff
and fold into the cheese mixture.

5 Pour the mixture over the cookie
shell in the prepared pan and
bake in a preheated oven, 350°F/
180°C, for 35–45 minutes, until just
set. Don't worry if it cracks or sinks—
this is quite normal.

6 Leave the cheesecake in the pan
to cool. Serve with fruit coulis
(see Cook's Tip).

honey & nut nests

serves four

8 oz/225 g dried angel hair pasta

½ cup butter

1½ cups chopped pistachios

½ cup sugar

⅓ cup honey

⅔ cup water

2 tsp lemon juice

salt

strained plain yogurt, to serve

COOK'S TIP

Angel hair pasta is also
known as capelli d'angelo. It is
long and very fine, and is usually
sold in small bunches that
resemble nests.

1 Bring a large pan of lightly salted
water to a boil. Add the pasta,
bring back to a boil, and cook for
8–10 minutes, or until tender but still
firm to the bite. Drain and return to the
pan. Add the butter and toss to coat
the pasta thoroughly. Let cool.

2 Arrange 4 small tart or poaching
rings on a cookie sheet. Divide
the angel hair pasta into 8 equal
portions and spoon 1 portion into each
ring. Press down lightly. Top the pasta
with half of the nuts, then add the
remaining pasta portions.

3 Bake in a preheated oven,
350°F/180°C, for 45 minutes,
or until golden brown.

4 Meanwhile, put the sugar, honey,
and water in a pan and bring to a
boil over low heat, stirring constantly,
until the sugar has dissolved. Simmer
for 10 minutes, add the lemon juice
and simmer for 5 minutes more.

5 Carefully transfer the angel hair
nests to a serving dish using a
spatula. Pour the honey syrup over
them, sprinkle with the remaining
pistachios, and let cool completely
before serving. Hand the strained plain
yogurt separately.

banana pies

DOUGH

3½ cups all-purpose flour, plus extra
    for dusting

4 tbsp shortening

4 tbsp sweet butter

½ cup water

FILLING

2 large bananas

⅓ cup finely chopped no-need-
    to-soak dried apricots

pinch of nutmeg

dash of orange juice

1 egg yolk, beaten

confectioners' sugar, for dusting

1 To make the dough, strain the
flour into a large mixing bowl.
Add the shortening and butter and rub
into the flour with your fingertips until
the mixture resembles bread crumbs.
Gradually blend in the water and bring
together with your fingers to form a
soft dough. Wrap in plastic wrap and
chill in the refrigerator for 30 minutes.

2 To make the filling, mash the
bananas in a bowl with a fork
and stir in the apricots, nutmeg, and
orange juice, mixing well.

3 Roll the dough out on a lightly
floured counter and stamp out
16 circles, 4 inches/10 cm wide.

4 Spoon a little banana filling onto
one half of each circle and fold
the dough over the filling to make
semicircles. Pinch the edges together
and seal by pressing with a fork.

5 Arrange the pies on a large
nonstick cookie sheet and brush
them with the beaten egg yolk. Cut a
small slit in the top of each pie, then
cook in a preheated oven, 350°F/
180°C, for about 25 minutes, or until
golden brown.

6 Dust the banana pies with
confectioners' sugar and serve.

chinese custard tarts

makes fifteen

DOUGH

1¼ cups all-purpose flour, plus extra
   for dusting

scant ¼ cup superfine sugar

4 tbsp sweet butter

2 tbsp shortening

2 tbsp water

CUSTARD

2 medium eggs

generous ¼ cup superfine sugar

¾ cup milk

½ tsp ground nutmeg, plus extra
   for sprinkling

cream, to serve

1 To make the dough, strain the flour into a bowl. Add the sugar and rub in the butter and shortening with your fingertips until the mixture resembles bread crumbs. Add the water and mix to form a firm dough.

2 Transfer the dough to a lightly floured counter and knead for 5 minutes, until smooth. Cover with plastic wrap and chill in the refrigerator while you are preparing the filling.

3 To make the custard, beat the eggs and sugar together. Gradually add the milk and ground nutmeg and beat until well blended.

4 Separate the dough into 15 even-size pieces. Flatten the dough pieces into circles and press into shallow muffin pans.

5 Spoon the custard into the tart shells and cook the tarts in a preheated oven, 300°F/150°C, for 25–30 minutes.

6 Transfer the Chinese custard tarts to a wire rack, let cool slightly, then sprinkle with nutmeg. Serve warm or cold with cream.

Cakes & Bread

There is nothing more traditional than morning coffee and cakes and this chapter gives a wickedly extravagant twist to some of those delicious classics—full of chocolate, spice, and all things nice, these recipes are a treat to enjoy. The chapter includes a variety of different cakes depending on the time you have and the effort you want to spend. Small cakes include Cranberry Muffins, Almond Slices, and Dark Biscuits. These cakes are easier to prepare and cook than larger ones and are particular favorites.

cinnamon & currant loaf

makes one loaf

⅔ cup butter, diced, plus extra
   for greasing

2¾ cups all-purpose flour

pinch of salt

1 tbsp baking powder

1 tbsp ground cinnamon

¾ cup brown sugar

¾ cup currants

finely grated rind of 1 orange

5–6 tbsp orange juice

6 tbsp milk

2 eggs, beaten lightly

1 Grease a 2-lb/900-g loaf pan with butter and line the base with baking parchment.

2 Strain the flour, salt, baking powder, and ground cinnamon into a bowl. Rub in the butter with your fingertips until the mixture resembles bread crumbs.

3 Stir in the sugar, currants, and orange rind. Beat the orange juice, milk, and eggs together and add to the dry ingredients. Mix well.

4 Spoon the mixture into the prepared pan. Make a dip in the center to help the loaf rise evenly.

5 Bake the loaf in a preheated oven, 350°F/180°C, for about 1–1 hour 10 minutes, or until a fine metal skewer inserted into the center of the loaf comes out clean.

6 Let the loaf cool before turning it out of the pan. Transfer to a wire rack and let cool completely before slicing.

COOK'S TIP

Once you have added the liquid to the dry ingredients, work as quickly as possible because the baking powder is activated by the liquid.

banana & cranberry loaf

makes one loaf

1 tbsp butter, for greasing

1¼ cups self-rising flour

½ tsp baking powder

¾ cup brown sugar

2 bananas, mashed

⅓ cup chopped candied peel

2 tbsp chopped mixed nuts

¼ cup dried cranberries

5–6 tbsp orange juice

2 eggs, beaten lightly

⅔ cup sunflower oil

¾ cup confectioners' sugar, strained

grated rind of 1 orange

COOK'S TIP

This tea bread will keep for a couple of days. Wrap it carefully and store in a cool, dry place.

---

1 Grease a 2-lb/900-g loaf pan with the butter and line the base with baking parchment.

2 Strain the flour and baking powder into a mixing bowl. Stir in the sugar, bananas, chopped candied peel, nuts, and cranberries.

3 Stir the orange juice, eggs, and oil together, until thoroughly blended. Add the mixture to the dry ingredients and mix well. Pour the mixture into the prepared pan and level the surface with a spatula.

4 Bake in a preheated oven, 350°F/180°C, for about 1 hour, until firm to the touch or until a fine metal skewer inserted into the center of the loaf comes out clean.

5 Turn out the loaf onto a wire rack and let cool completely.

6 Mix the confectioners' sugar with a little water and drizzle the frosting over the loaf. Sprinkle orange rind over the top. Let the frosting set before serving the loaf in slices.

banana & date loaf

makes one loaf

⅓ cup butter, diced, plus extra
   for greasing
generous 1½ cups self-rising flour
⅓ cup superfine sugar
⅔ cup chopped pitted dried dates
2 bananas, mashed coarsely
2 eggs, beaten lightly
2 tbsp honey

COOK'S TIP

This tea bread will keep for
several days if stored in an
airtight container and kept
in a cool, dry place.

VARIATION

Substitute other dried fruit, such
as prunes or apricots, for the
dates. Use no-soak varieties for
the best results.

1 Grease a 2-lb/900-g loaf pan and
line with baking parchment.

2 Strain the flour into a mixing
bowl. Rub the butter into the flour
with your fingertips until the mixture
resembles fine bread crumbs.

3 Add the sugar, chopped dates,
bananas, beaten eggs, and honey
to the dry ingredients. Mix together to
form a pourable consistency.

4 Spoon the mixture into the
prepared loaf pan and level the
surface with a spatula.

5 Bake the loaf in a preheated
oven, 325°F/160°C for about,
1 hour, or until golden brown and a
fine metal skewer inserted into the
center of the loaf comes out clean.

6 Let the loaf cool for 10 minutes
before turning out of the pan,
then transfer to a wire rack to cool.

7 Serve the loaf warm or cold, cut
into thick slices.

fruit loaf with apple spread

makes one loaf

1 tbsp butter, for greasing

2 cups rolled oats

1 tsp ground cinnamon

½ cup light brown sugar

⅔ cup golden raisins

1 cup seedless raisins

2 tbsp malt extract

1¼ cups unsweetened apple juice

1¼ cups whole-wheat flour

3 tsp baking powder

FRUIT SPREAD

1½ cups strawberries, washed
    and hulled

2 eating apples, cored, chopped,
    and mixed with 1 tbsp
    lemon juice

1¼ cups unsweetened
    apple juice

TO SERVE

strawberries

apple wedges

1 Grease and line a 2-lb/900-g loaf pan. Place the oats, sugar, cinnamon, raisins, and malt extract in a bowl. Pour in the apple juice, stir, and let soak for 30 minutes.

2 Strain in the flour and baking powder, adding any bran that remains in the strainer, and fold in using a metal spoon.

3 Spoon the mixture into the pan and bake in a preheated oven, 350°F/180°C, for 1½ hours, until a fine metal skewer inserted into the center of the loaf comes out clean.

4 Let the loaf stand for 10 minutes, then turn out onto a wire rack and let cool completely.

5 Meanwhile, to make the fruit spread, place the strawberries and apples in a pan and pour in the apple juice. Bring the mixture to a boil,

cover, and simmer gently for 30 minutes. Beat the sauce well, then spoon into a sterilized, warmed jar. Let the sauce cool completely, then seal and label the jar.

6 Serve the fruit loaf cut into slices with 1–2 tablespoons of the fruit spread and an assortment of strawberries and apple wedges.

cranberry muffins

makes eighteen

1 tbsp butter, for greasing

generous 1½ cups all-purpose flour

2 tsp baking powder

½ tsp salt

¼ cup superfine sugar

4 tbsp butter, melted

2 eggs, beaten lightly

generous ¾ cup milk

1 cup fresh cranberries

scant ½ cup freshly grated
  Parmesan cheese

1 Lightly grease 2 muffin pans with a little butter. Strain the flour, baking powder, and salt into a mixing bowl. Stir in the superfine sugar.

2 In a separate bowl, combine the butter, beaten eggs, and milk, then pour into the bowl of dry ingredients. Mix lightly together until all of the ingredients are evenly blended, then stir in the cranberries.

3 Divide the mixture among the prepared pans.

4 Sprinkle the grated Parmesan cheese over the top of each portion of the muffin mixture.

5 Bake in a preheated oven, 400°F/200°C, for 20 minutes, or until the muffins are well risen and golden brown.

6 Let the muffins cool slightly in the pans for 10 minutes, then transfer them to a wire rack, and let cool completely.

date & honey loaf

makes one loaf

1 tbsp butter, for greasing

1¾ cups strong white bread flour

½ cup brown bread flour

½ tsp salt

1 envelope active dry yeast

generous ¾ cup lukewarm water

3 tbsp sunflower oil

3 tbsp honey

½ cup chopped pitted dates

2 tbsp sesame seeds

COOK'S TIP

If you cannot find a warm place, sit a bowl with the dough in it over a pan of warm water and cover.

---

1 Grease a 2-lb/900-g loaf pan with the butter.

2 Strain both types of flour into a large mixing bowl, and stir in the salt and dry yeast. Pour in the lukewarm water, sunflower oil, and honey. Bring together to form a dough.

3 Place the dough on a lightly floured counter and knead for about 5 minutes, until smooth.

4 Place the dough in a greased bowl, cover, and let rise in a warm place for about 1 hour, or until doubled in size.

5 Knead in the dates and sesame seeds. Shape the dough and place in the pan.

6 Cover and stand in a warm place for a further 30 minutes, or until springy to the touch.

7 Bake in a preheated oven, 425°F/220°C, for 30 minutes. When the loaf is cooked, it should sound hollow when tapped.

8 Transfer the loaf to a wire rack and let cool completely. Serve cut into thick slices.

mango twist bread

makes one loaf

3 tbsp butter, diced, plus extra
for greasing

3½ cups strong white bread flour,
plus extra for dusting

1 tsp salt

1 envelope active dry yeast

1 tsp ground ginger

¼ cup brown sugar

1 small mango, peeled, pitted, and
blended to a paste

1 cup lukewarm water

2 tbsp honey

⅔ cup golden raisins

1 egg, beaten lightly

confectioners' sugar, for dusting

1 Grease a cookie sheet with a little butter. Strain the flour and salt into a mixing bowl, stir in the dry yeast, ginger, and brown sugar and rub in the butter with your fingertips until the mixture resembles bread crumbs.

2 Stir in the mango paste, lukewarm water, and honey and bring together to form a dough.

3 Place the dough on a lightly floured counter. Knead for about 5 minutes, until smooth. Alternatively, use an electric mixer with a dough hook. Place the dough in a greased bowl, cover, and let rise in a warm place for about 1 hour, until it has doubled in size.

4 Knead in the golden raisins and shape the dough into 2 sausage shapes, each 10 inches/25 cm long. Carefully twist the 2 pieces together and pinch the ends to seal. Place the dough on the cookie sheet, cover, and leave in a warm place for another 40 minutes.

5 Brush the loaf with the egg and bake in a preheated oven, 425°F/220°C, for 30 minutes, or until golden. Let cool on a wire rack. Dust with confectioners' sugar before serving.

COOK'S TIP
You can tell when the bread is cooked because it will sound hollow when tapped.

citrus bread

makes one loaf

4 tbsp butter, diced, plus extra
    for greasing

3½ cups strong white bread flour,
    plus extra for dusting

½ tsp salt

¼ cup superfine sugar

1 envelope active dry yeast

5–6 tbsp orange juice

4 tbsp lemon juice

3–4 tbsp lime juice

⅔ cup lukewarm water

1 orange

1 lemon

1 lime

2 tbsp honey, for glazing

1 Lightly grease a cookie sheet with a little butter.

2 Strain the flour and salt into a large mixing bowl. Stir in the sugar and dry yeast.

3 Rub in the butter with your fingertips until the mixture resembles bread crumbs. Add all of the fruit juices and the water and bring together with your fingers to form a dough.

4 Place the dough on a lightly floured counter and knead for 5 minutes. Alternatively, use an electric mixer with a dough hook. Place the dough in a greased bowl, cover, and let rise in a warm place for 1 hour, until doubled in size.

5 Meanwhile, grate the rind of the orange, lemon, and lime. Knead the fruit rinds into the dough.

6 Divide the dough into 2 balls, making one slightly bigger than the other.

7 Place the larger ball on the cookie sheet and set the smaller one on top.

8 Push a floured finger through the center of the dough. Cover and let rise for about 40 minutes, or until springy to the touch.

9 Bake in a preheated oven, 425°F/220°C, for 35 minutes. Remove from the oven and transfer to a wire rack. Glaze with the honey and let cool completely.

crown loaf

makes one loaf

2 tbsp butter, diced, plus extra
   for greasing
generous 1½ cups strong white
   bread flour, plus extra for dusting
½ tsp salt
1 envelope active dry yeast
½ cup lukewarm milk
1 egg, beaten lightly
FILLING
4 tbsp butter, softened
¼ cup brown sugar
2 tbsp chopped hazelnuts
1 tbsp chopped preserved ginger
⅓ cup candied peel
1 cup confectioners' sugar
2 tbsp lemon juice

1 Grease a cookie sheet with a little butter. Strain the flour and salt into a large mixing bowl. Stir in the yeast. Rub in the butter with your fingertips. Add the milk and egg and bring together with your fingers to form a dough.

2 Place the dough in a greased bowl, cover, and stand in a warm place for about 40 minutes, until doubled in size. Punch down the dough lightly for 1 minute, then roll out into a rectangle measuring 12 x 9 inches/30 x 23 cm.

3 To make the filling, cream the butter and sugar together in a large bowl until light and fluffy. Stir in the hazelnuts, ginger, candied peel, and rum or brandy. Spread the filling over the dough, leaving a 1-inch/2.5-cm border around the edges.

4 Roll up the dough, starting from one of the long edges, into a sausage shape. Cut into slices at 2-inch/5-cm intervals and place the slices in a circle on the cookie sheet, sides just touching. Cover and stand in a warm place to rise for 30 minutes.

5 Bake in a preheated oven, 325°F/190°C, for 20–30 minutes or until golden. Meanwhile, mix the confectioners' sugar with enough lemon juice to form a thin frosting.

6 Let the loaf cool slightly before drizzling with frosting. Let the frosting set slightly before serving.

chocolate bread

makes one loaf

1 tbsp butter, for greasing

3½ cups strong white bread flour,
   plus extra for dusting

¼ cup unsweetened cocoa

1 tsp salt

1 envelope active dry yeast

2 tbsp brown sugar

1 tbsp oil

1¼ cups lukewarm water

1 Lightly grease a 2-lb/900-g loaf pan with the butter.

2 Strain the flour and unsweetened cocoa into a mixing bowl. Stir in the salt, dry yeast, and sugar.

3 Pour in the oil with the water and mix the ingredients together to form a dough.

4 Place the dough on a lightly floured counter and knead for 5 minutes. Alternatively, use an electric mixer with a dough hook.

5 Place the dough in a greased bowl, cover, and let rise in a warm place for about 1 hour, or until it has doubled in size.

6 Punch down the dough lightly for 1 minute, then shape it into a loaf. Place in the prepared pan, cover, and let rise in a warm place for another 30 minutes.

7 Bake in a preheated oven, 400°F/200°C, for 25–30 minutes. When the loaf is cooked, it should sound hollow when tapped on the base.

8 Transfer the bread to a wire rack and let cool completely. Cut into slices and serve .

cinnamon swirls

makes twelve

2 tbsp butter, diced, plus extra
    for greasing
generous 1½ cups strong white
    bread flour, plus extra for dusting
½ tsp salt
1 envelope active dry yeast
1 egg, beaten lightly
½ cup lukewarm milk
2 tbsp maple syrup
FILLING
4 tbsp butter, softened
2 tsp ground cinnamon
¼ cup brown sugar
⅓ cup currants

1 Grease a 9-inch/23-cm square baking pan with a little butter.

2 Strain the flour and salt into a mixing bowl. Stir in the dry yeast. Rub in the butter with your fingertips until the mixture resembles bread crumbs. Add the egg and milk and bring together with your fingers to form a dough.

3 Form the dough into a ball, place in a greased bowl, cover, and let stand in a warm place for about 40 minutes, or until doubled in size.

4 Punch down the dough lightly for 1 minute, then roll out to a rectangle measuring 12 x 9 inches/ 30 x 23 cm.

5 To make the filling, cream the softened butter, cinnamon, and brown sugar together in a bowl until light and fluffy. Spread the filling evenly over the dough rectangle, leaving a 1-inch/2.5-cm border around the edges. Sprinkle the currants evenly over the top.

6 Roll up the dough from one of the long edges, and press down to seal. Cut the roll into 12 slices. Place them in the pan, cover, and let rise in a warm place for 30 minutes.

7 Bake in a preheated oven, 375°F/190°C, for 20–30 minutes, or until well risen. Brush with the syrup and let cool slightly before serving.

69

crunchy fruit cake

serves eight

⅓ cup butter, softened, plus extra
  for greasing
½ cup superfine sugar
2 eggs, beaten lightly
generous ⅓ cup self-rising
  flour, strained
1 tsp baking powder
⅔ cup cornmeal
1⅓ cups mixed dried fruit
¼ cup pine nuts
grated rind of 1 lemon
4 tbsp lemon juice
2 tbsp milk

VARIATION

To give a crumblier, lighter fruit
cake, omit the cornmeal and use
a generous 1 cup of self-rising
flour instead.

---

1 Grease a 7-inch/18-cm cake pan
  with a little butter and line the
base with baking parchment.

2 Whisk the butter and sugar
  together in a bowl until light
and fluffy.

3 Whisk in the beaten eggs, a little
  at a time, whisking thoroughly
after each addition.

4 Gently fold the flour, baking
  powder, and cornmeal into the
mixture until well blended.

5 Stir in the mixed dried fruit, pine
  nuts, grated lemon rind, lemon
juice, and milk.

6 Spoon the mixture into the pan
  and level the surface.

7 Bake in a preheated oven,
  350°F/180°C, for about 1 hour, or
until a fine metal skewer inserted into
the center of the cake comes out clean.

8 Let the cake cool in the pan
  before turning out.

clementine cake

serves eight

¾ cup butter, softened, plus extra
   for greasing

2 clementines

¾ cup superfine sugar

3 eggs, beaten lightly

1¼ cups self-rising flour

3 tbsp ground almonds

3 tbsp light cream

GLAZE AND TOPPING

6 tbsp clementine juice

2 tbsp superfine sugar

3 white sugar lumps, crushed

COOK'S TIP

If you like, chop the rind
from the clementines in a
food processor or blender
with the sugar in step 2. Tip
the mixture into a bowl
with the butter and begin
to cream the mixture.

1 Grease a 7-inch/18-cm round pan
with a little butter and line the
base with baking parchment.

2 Pare the rind from the clementines
and chop it finely. Cream the
butter, sugar, and clementine rind
together in a bowl until pale and fluffy.

3 Gradually add the beaten eggs to
the mixture, beating thoroughly
after each addition.

4 Gently fold in the flour, ground
almonds, and light cream. Spoon
the mixture into the prepared pan.

5 Bake in a preheated oven,
350°F/180°C, for 55–60 minutes,
or until a fine metal skewer inserted
into the center comes out clean. Let
cool for 10 minutes.

6 Meanwhile, to make the glaze,
put the clementine juice into a
small pan with the superfine sugar.
Bring to a boil over low heat and
simmer for 5 minutes.

7 Turn out the cake onto a wire
rack. Drizzle the glaze over the
cake until it has been absorbed and
sprinkle with the crushed sugar lumps.
Let cool completely before serving.

caraway madeira

serves eight

1 cup butter, softened, plus extra
 for greasing

scant 1 cup brown sugar

3 eggs, beaten lightly

2½ cups self-rising flour

1 tbsp caraway seeds

grated rind of 1 lemon

6 tbsp milk

1 or 2 strips of citron peel

1 Grease a 2-lb/900-g loaf pan and line with baking parchment.

2 Cream the butter and brown sugar together in a bowl until pale and fluffy.

3 Gradually add the beaten eggs to the creamed mixture, beating well after each addition.

4 Strain the flour into the bowl and gently fold into the creamed mixture with a figure-eight movement.

5 Add the caraway seeds, lemon rind, and milk, and gently fold in until thoroughly blended.

6 Spoon the mixture into the prepared pan and level the surface with a spatula.

7 Bake in a preheated oven, 325°F/160°C, for 20 minutes.

8 Remove the cake from the oven and gently place the pieces of citron peel on top. Return to the oven and bake for 40 minutes more, or until the cake is well risen, golden, and a fine skewer inserted into the center comes out clean.

9 Let the cake cool in the pan for 10 minutes before turning out, then transfer it to a wire rack to let it cool completely.

COOK'S TIP

Citron peel is available in the
baking section of large stores.
If it is unavailable, you can
substitute chopped mixed peel.

orange kugelhopf cake

serves four

1 cup butter, softened, plus extra
  for greasing
generous 1 cup superfine sugar
4 eggs, separated
scant 3½ cups all-purpose flour
pinch of salt
3 tsp baking powder
1¼ cups fresh orange juice
1 tbsp orange flower water
1 tsp grated orange rind
SYRUP
¾ cup orange juice
1 cup granulated sugar

1 Grease and flour a 10-inch/25-cm
kugelhopf pan or deep ring mold.

2 Cream the butter and superfine
sugar together in a bowl until
light and fluffy, then add the egg
yolks, 1 at a time, whisking well after
each addition.

3 Strain the flour, salt, and baking
powder into a separate bowl.
Fold the dry ingredients and the
orange juice alternately into the
creamed mixture with a metal spoon,
working as lightly as possible. Gently
stir in the orange flower water and
orange rind.

4 Whisk the egg whites until they
form soft peaks, then gently fold
them into the mixture using a figure-
eight movement.

5 Pour into the prepared pan or
mold. Bake in a preheated oven,
350°F/180°C, for 50–55 minutes, or
until a fine metal skewer inserted into
the center of the cake comes out clean.

6 To make the syrup, bring the
orange juice and sugar to a boil
in a small pan over low heat, then
simmer gently for 5 minutes, until the
sugar has dissolved.

7 Remove the cake from the
oven and let cool in the pan for
10 minutes. Prick the top of the cake
with a fine metal skewer and brush
over half of the syrup. Let the cake
cool, still in the pan, for another
10 minutes, then invert the cake
onto a wire rack placed over a deep
plate and brush the syrup over the
cake until it is completely covered.
Serve warm or cold.

lemon syrup cake

serves eight

1 tbsp butter, for greasing

scant 1½ cups all-purpose flour

2 tsp baking powder

1 cup superfine sugar

4 eggs

⅔ cup sour cream

grated rind of 1 large lemon

4 tbsp lemon juice

⅔ cup sunflower oil

SYRUP

4 tbsp confectioners' sugar

3 tbsp lemon juice

1 Lightly grease an 8-inch/20-cm loose-based round cake pan with a little butter and line the base with baking parchment.

2 Strain the flour and baking powder into a large mixing bowl and stir in the sugar.

3 In a bowl or pitcher, whisk the eggs, sour cream, lemon rind, lemon juice, and oil together.

4 Pour the egg mixture into the dry ingredients and mix well until evenly blended.

5 Pour the mixture into the prepared pan and bake in a preheated oven, 350°F/180°C, for 45–60 minutes, until risen and golden on top.

6 To make the syrup, mix the confectioners' sugar and lemon juice together in a small pan. Stir over low heat until just starting to bubble and turn syrupy.

7 As soon as the cake comes out of the oven prick the surface with a fine metal skewer, then brush the syrup over the top. Let cool completely in the pan before turning out and serving.

COOK'S TIP

Pricking the surface of the hot cake with a skewer insures that the syrup seeps into the cake and the flavor is absorbed.

apple cake with cider

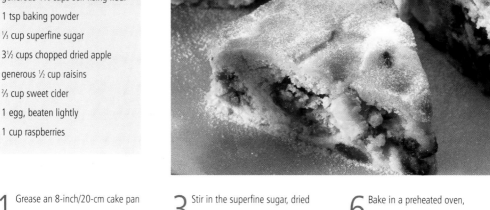

1 Grease an 8-inch/20-cm cake pan with a little butter and line with baking parchment.

2 Strain the flour and baking powder into a large mixing bowl and rub in the butter with your fingertips until the mixture resembles fine bread crumbs.

3 Stir in the superfine sugar, dried apple, and raisins.

4 Pour in the sweet cider and egg and mix together until thoroughly blended. Stir in the raspberries very gently so that they do not break up.

5 Pour the mixture into the prepared cake pan.

6 Bake in a preheated oven, 375°F/190°C, for 40 minutes, or until risen and lightly golden.

7 Let the cake cool in the pan for 10 minutes, then turn out onto a wire rack, and let cool completely before serving

rich fruit cake

serves four

1 tbsp butter, for greasing

generous ½ cup no-soak prunes

1 cup chopped pitted dates

generous ¾ cup unsweetened
  orange juice

2 tbsp molasses

1 tsp finely grated lemon rind

1 tsp finely grated orange rind

generous 1½ cups whole-
  wheat flour

2 tsp baking powder

1 tsp allspice

⅔ cup seedless raisins

⅔ cup golden raisins

⅔ cup currants

generous 1 cup dried cranberries

3 extra large eggs, separated

TO DECORATE

1 tbsp apricot preserve, warmed

confectioners' sugar, for dusting

generous 1 cup sugarpaste

strips of orange rind

strips of lemon rind

1 Grease a deep round 8-inch/20-cm cake pan and line with baking parchment. Chop the prunes, place in a pan with the dates, pour over the orange juice, and simmer over low heat for 10 minutes. Remove from the heat and beat to a paste. Stir in the molasses and rinds. Let cool.

2 Strain the flour, baking powder and allspice into a bowl, adding any bran from the strainer. Add the dried fruits. When the prune mixture is cool, whisk in the egg yolks. In a separate bowl, whisk the egg whites until stiff. Spoon the fruit mixture into the dry ingredients and mix together.

3 Gently fold in the egg whites using a metal spoon. Transfer to the prepared cake pan and bake in a preheated oven, 325°F/170°C, for 1½ hours. Let cool in the pan

4 Turn the cake out and brush the top with apricot preserve. Dust the counter with confectioners' sugar and roll out the sugarpaste thinly. Lay the sugarpaste over the top of the cake and trim the edges. Decorate with citrus rind.

carrot & ginger cake

serves ten

1 tbsp butter, for greasing

generous 1½ cups all-purpose flour

1 tsp baking powder

1 tsp baking soda

2 tsp ground ginger

½ tsp salt

scant 1 cup light brown sugar

generous 1 cup grated carrots

2 pieces of preserved
   ginger, chopped

1 tbsp grated fresh gingerroot

⅓ cup seedless raisins

2 eggs, beaten lightly

3 tbsp corn oil

juice of 1 orange

FROSTING

1 cup lowfat soft cheese

4 tbsp confectioners' sugar

1 tsp vanilla extract

TO DECORATE

grated carrot

finely chopped preserved ginger

ground ginger

1 Grease an 8-inch/20-cm round cake pan with butter and line with baking parchment.

2 Strain the flour, baking powder, baking soda, ground ginger, and salt into a bowl. Stir in the sugar, carrots, preserved ginger, fresh ginger, and raisins. In a separate bowl, beat together the eggs, oil, and orange juice, then stir into the dry ingredients.

3 Spoon the mixture into the prepared pan and bake in a preheated oven, 350°F/180°C, for 1–1¼ hours, until firm to the touch, or until a fine metal skewer inserted into the center of the cake comes out clean. Let cool in the pan

4 To make the frosting, place the soft cheese in a bowl and beat to soften. Sift in the confectioners' sugar and add the vanilla extract. Mix well.

5 Turn the cake out and smooth the frosting over the top. Decorate with grated carrot and preserved and ground ginger and serve.

strawberry roulade

serves eight

3 extra large eggs

⅔ cup superfine sugar

scant 1 cup all-purpose flour

1 tbsp hot water

FILLING

¾ cup mascarpone

1 tsp almond extract

1½ cups small strawberries

TO DECORATE

1 tbsp toasted sliced almonds

1 tsp confectioners' sugar

1 Line a 14 x 10-inch/35 x 25-cm jelly roll pan with baking parchment. Place the eggs in a heatproof bowl with the superfine sugar. Whisk together, then place the bowl over a pan of hot water and whisk the mixture until pale and thick.

2 Remove the bowl from the pan. Strain in the flour and fold into the egg mixture with the hot water. Pour the mixture into the prepared pan and bake in a preheated oven, 425°F/220°C, for 8–10 minutes, until golden and set.

3 Remove from the oven and turn out the roulade onto a sheet of baking parchment. Peel off the lining paper and roll up the sponge cake tightly along with the baking parchment. Wrap in a dish towel and let cool.

4 To make the filling, mix together the mascarpone and almond extract. Reserve a few strawberries for decoration, then wash, hull, and slice the rest. Chill the mascarpone mixture and the strawberries in the refrigerator until required.

5 Unroll the cake, spread the mascarpone mixture over the surface, and sprinkle with sliced strawberries. Roll the cake up again and transfer to a serving plate. Sprinkle with almonds and lightly dust with confectioners' sugar. Decorate with the reserved strawberries.

orange & almond cake

serves eight

1 tbsp butter, for greasing

4 eggs, separated

scant ¾ cup superfine sugar

finely grated rind and juice
  of 2 oranges

finely grated rind and juice
  of 1 lemon

generous 1 cup ground almonds

2½ tbsp self-rising flour

ORANGE-CINNAMON CREAM

generous ¾ cup whipping cream

1 tsp ground cinnamon

2 tsp caster sugar

TO DECORATE

1 tbsp toasted sliced almonds

confectioners' sugar, for dusting

VARIATION

You could serve this cake with a
syrup. Boil the juice and grated
rind of 2 oranges with scant
⅓ cup superfine sugar and
2 tablespoons of water for
5–6 minutes until slightly
thickened. Stir in 1 tablespoon
orange liqueur before serving.

1 Grease a deep 7-inch/18-cm round cake pan with butter. Line the base with baking parchment.

2 Cream the egg yolks and sugar in a bowl until the mixture is pale and thick. Whisk half of the orange rind and all of the lemon rind into the egg yolk mixture.

COOK'S TIP

When whipping cream, chill the
bowl, whisk, and cream before
starting. Whisk briskly until it
starts to thicken and then more
slowly until soft peaks form.

3 Mix the juice from the oranges and lemon with the ground almonds and stir into the egg yolk mixture. Gently fold in the flour.

4 Whisk the egg whites until stiff, then gently fold them into the egg yolk mixture.

5 Pour the mixture into the prepared pan and bake in a preheated oven, 350°F/180°C, for 35–40 minutes, or until golden and springy to the touch. Let cool in the pan for 10 minutes, then turn out and leave to cool completely.

6 Whip the cream until soft peaks form. Stir in the remaining orange rind, cinnamon and sugar. Cover the cooled cake with the sliced almonds, dust with confectioners' sugar, and serve immediately with the orange and cinnamon cream.

coconut cake

serves six—eight

½ cup butter, diced, plus extra
   for greasing
generous 1½ cups self-rising flour
pinch of salt
½ cup raw brown sugar
1 cup dry unsweetened coconut,
   plus extra for sprinkling
2 eggs, beaten lightly
4 tbsp milk

2 Strain the flour and salt into a
  mixing bowl and rub in the butter
with your fingertips until the mixture
resembles fine bread crumbs.

3 Stir in the sugar, coconut, eggs,
  and milk and mix to a soft
pourable consistency.

1 Lightly grease a 2-lb/900-g loaf
  pan with butter and line with
baking parchment.

4 Spoon the mixture into the
  prepared loaf pan and level the
surface with a spatula. Bake in a
preheated oven, 325°F/160°C, for
30 minutes.

5 Remove the cake from the
  oven and sprinkle with the extra
coconut. Return to the oven and bake
for 30 minutes more, until risen and
golden and a metal skewer inserted
into the center comes out clean.

6 Let the cake cool slightly in the
  pan, then turn out, and transfer
to a wire rack, and let cool completely
before serving.

almond slices

makes eight

3 eggs

⅔ cup ground almonds

1½ cups dry milk

1 cup granulated sugar

½ tsp saffron threads

scant ½ cup sweet butter

1 tbsp sliced almonds, to decorate

1 Beat the eggs together in a bowl and set aside.

2 Place the ground almonds, dry milk, sugar, and saffron in a large mixing bowl and mix well.

3 Melt the butter in a small pan over low heat. Pour the melted butter over the dry ingredients and mix well until thoroughly blended.

4 Add the reserved beaten eggs to the mixture and mix well.

5 Spread the cake mixture evenly in a shallow 7–9-inch/15–20-cm ovenproof dish and bake in a preheated oven, 325°F/160°C, for

COOK'S TIP

These almond slices are best eaten hot, but they may also be served cold. They can be made a day or even a week in advance and reheated. They also freeze beautifully.

45 minutes, or until a fine metal skewer inserted into the center of the cake comes out clean.

6 Cut the almond cake into 8 slices. Decorate the almond slices with sliced almonds, and transfer to serving plates. Serve hot or cold.

pear & ginger cake

serves six

scant 1 cup sweet butter, softened,
    plus extra for greasing
generous ¾ cup superfine sugar
1¼ cups self-rising flour, strained
1 tbsp ground ginger
3 eggs, beaten lightly
1 lb/450 g pears, peeled, cored,
    and thinly sliced, then brushed
    with lemon juice
1 tbsp brown sugar
ice cream or heavy cream, lightly
    whipped, to serve (optional)

COOK'S TIP

Store brown sugar in an airtight
container, rather than in its
package, where it can absorb
water from the air. If the sugar
becomes hard, do not throw it
away. Wrap the package in a
clean, damp dish towel and heat
in the microwave on Medium
for 1–2 minutes, until it begins
to soften.

1 Lightly grease a deep 8-inch/ 20-cm cake pan with butter and line the base with baking parchment.

2 Mix all but 2 tablespoons of the butter with the superfine sugar, flour, ginger, and eggs in a bowl. Beat with a whisk until the mixture forms a smooth consistency.

3 Spoon the cake batter into the prepared pan and level out the surface with a spatula.

4 Arrange the pear slices over the cake batter. Sprinkle with the brown sugar and dot with the remaining butter.

5 Bake in a preheated oven, 350°F/180°C, for 35–40 minutes, or until the cake is golden on top and feels springy to the touch.

6 Serve the pear and ginger cake warm, with ice cream or whipped cream, if you like.

VARIATION

For a different flavor, substitute 2
teaspoons ground cinnamon for
the ground ginger and use
vanilla sugar instead of plain.

coffee streusel cake

serves eight

½ cup butter, melted and cooled,
    plus extra for greasing

2 cups all-purpose flour

1 tbsp baking powder

⅓ cup superfine sugar

⅔ cup milk

2 eggs

2 tbsp instant coffee mixed with
    1 tbsp boiling water

⅓ cup chopped almonds

confectioners' sugar, for dusting

TOPPING

½ cup self-rising flour

⅓ cup raw brown sugar

2 tbsp butter, diced

1 tsp ground allspice

1 tbsp water

1 Grease a 9-inch/23-cm loose-based round cake pan with butter and line with baking parchment. Strain the flour and baking powder into a mixing bowl, then stir in the superfine sugar.

2 Whisk the milk, eggs, melted butter, and coffee mixture together and pour onto the dry ingredients. Add the chopped almonds and mix lightly together. Spoon the mixture into the prepared pan.

3 To make the topping, combine the flour and raw brown sugar in a bowl.

4 Rub in the butter with your fingertips until the mixture resembles bread crumbs. Sprinkle in the allspice and water and bring the mixture together into loose crumbs. Sprinkle evenly over the cake batter.

5 Bake the cake in a preheated oven, 375°F/190°C, for about 50 minutes–1 hour. Cover loosely with foil if the topping starts to brown too quickly. Let the cake cool in the pan, then turn out, dust with confectioners' sugar, and serve.

gingerbread

VARIATION

If you enjoy the flavor of ginger, try adding 1 tablespoon finely chopped preserved ginger to the mixture in step 3.

---

1 Grease a 9-inch/23-cm square cake pan with a little butter and line with baking parchment.

2 Melt the butter, sugar, and molasses in a pan over low heat. Remove from the heat and let cool.

3 Strain the flour, baking powder, baking soda, and ground ginger together into a mixing bowl.

4 Stir in the milk, egg, and cooled butter and molasses mixture, followed by the chopped apples.

5 Stir gently, then pour the mixture into the prepared pan, and level the surface with a spatula.

6 Bake in a preheated oven, 325°F/160°C, for 30–35 minutes, until the cake has risen and a fine metal skewer inserted into the center comes out clean.

7 Let the ginger cake cool in the pan, then turn out, and cut into 12 bars.

cherry biscuits

makes eight

6 tbsp butter, diced, plus extra
   for greasing
generous 1½ cups self-rising flour,
   plus extra for dusting
1 tbsp superfine sugar
pinch of salt
3 tbsp candied cherries, chopped
3 tbsp golden raisins
1 egg, beaten lightly
scant ¼ cup milk

COOK'S TIP
These biscuits will freeze
very successfully, but they
are best thawed and eaten
within 1 month.

1 Lightly grease a cookie sheet with a little butter.

2 Strain the flour, sugar, and salt into a mixing bowl and rub in the butter with your fingertips until the mixture resembles bread crumbs.

3 Stir in the candied cherries and golden raisins. Add the egg.

4 Reserve 1 tablespoon of the milk for glazing, then add the remainder to the mixture. Bring together to form a soft dough.

5 Roll out the dough on a lightly floured counter to a thickness of ¾ inch/2 cm and cut out 8 circles, using a 2-inch/5-cm cutter.

6 Place the biscuits on the prepared cookie sheet and brush the tops with the reserved milk.

7 Bake in a preheated oven, 425°F/220°C, for 8–10 minutes, or until the biscuits are golden brown.

8 Transfer the biscuits to a wire rack and let cool. Serve split in half and spread with butter.

dark biscuits

makes eight

6 tbsp butter, diced, plus extra
   for greasing
generous 1½ cups self-rising flour,
   plus extra for dusting
pinch of salt
1 tbsp superfine sugar
1 eating apple, peeled, cored,
   and chopped
1 egg, beaten lightly
2 tbsp molasses
5 tbsp milk

1 Lightly grease a cookie sheet with a little butter.

2 Strain the flour, sugar, and salt into a mixing bowl.

3 Add the butter and rub it in with your fingertips until the mixture resembles fine bread crumbs.

4 Stir the apple into the mixture until thoroughly combined.

5 Combine the beaten egg, molasses, and milk in a pitcher. Add to the dry ingredients and bring together to form a soft dough.

6 Roll out the dough on a lightly floured counter to a thickness of ¾ inch/2 cm and stamp out 8 circles, using a 2-inch/5-cm cutter.

7 Arrange the biscuits on the prepared cookie sheet and bake in a preheated oven, 425°F/220°C, for about 8–10 minutes.

8 Transfer the biscuits to a wire rack and let cool slightly. Serve split in half and spread with butter

apple shortcakes

serves four

2 tbsp butter, diced, plus extra
    for greasing

1¼ cups all-purpose flour, plus extra
    for dusting

½ tsp salt

1 tsp baking powder

1 tbsp superfine sugar

¼ cup milk

confectioners' sugar, for
    dusting (optional)

FILLING

3 eating apples, peeled, cored,
    and sliced

½ cup superfine sugar

1 tbsp lemon juice

1 tsp ground cinnamon

1¼ cups water

⅔ cup heavy cream, whipped lightly

1 Lightly grease a cookie sheet with a little butter. Strain the flour, salt, and baking powder into a mixing bowl. Stir in the sugar, then rub in the butter with your fingertips until the mixture resembles fine bread crumbs.

2 Pour in the milk and bring together to form a soft dough. Knead the dough lightly on a lightly

floured counter, then roll out to ½ inch/ 1 cm thick. Stamp out 4 circles, using a 2-inch/5-cm cutter. Transfer the circles to the prepared cookie sheet.

3 Bake in a preheated oven, 425°F/220°C, for 15 minutes, until risen and browned. Let cool.

4 To make the filling, place the apple slices, sugar, lemon juice, and cinnamon in a pan. Add the water, bring to a boil, and simmer, uncovered, for 5–10 minutes, until the apples are tender. Let cool a little, then remove the apples.

5 Split the shortcakes in half. Place each lower half on a serving plate and spoon a fourth of the apple slices onto each, and top with cream. Place the other half of the shortcake on top. Serve dusted with confectioners' sugar if you like.

sugar-topped blackberry & apple cake

serves ten

1 tbsp butter, for greasing

12 oz/350 g cooking apples

3 tbsp lemon juice

generous 2 cups whole-
wheat flour

2½ tsp baking powder

1 tsp ground cinnamon, plus extra
for dusting

1 cup prepared blackberries,
thawed if frozen, plus extra
to decorate

scant 1 cup light brown sugar

1 egg, beaten lightly

¾ cup lowfat plain yogurt

2 oz/55 g white or brown sugar
lumps, crushed lightly

sliced eating apple, to decorate

VARIATION

Try replacing the blackberries
with blueberries. Use the canned
or frozen variety if fresh
blueberries are unavailable.

---

1 Grease a 2-lb/900-g loaf pan with a little butter and line with baking parchment. Core, peel, and finely dice the cooking apples. Place them in a pan with the lemon juice, bring to a boil, cover, and simmer for 10 minutes, until soft. Beat well. Set aside to cool.

2 Strain the flour, baking powder, and cinnamon into a bowl, adding any bran that remains in the strainer. Stir in ⅔ cup of the blackberries and the sugar.

3 Make a well in the center of the ingredients and add the egg, yogurt, and cooled apple paste. Mix until thoroughly blended. Spoon the mixture into the prepared loaf pan and level over the top with a spatula.

4 Sprinkle with the remaining blackberries, pressing them down into the cake batter, and top the batter with the crushed sugar lumps. Bake in a preheated oven, 375°F/ 190°C, for 40–45 minutes, then let cool in the pan.

5 Turn the cake out and peel away the baking parchment. Serve dusted with cinnamon and decorated with blackberries and apple slices.

spicy bread

makes one loaf

2 tbsp butter, diced, plus extra
    for greasing
generous 1½ cups self-rising flour
¾ cup all-purpose flour, plus extra
    for dusting
1 tsp baking powder
¼ tsp salt
¼ tsp cayenne pepper
2 tsp curry powder
2 tsp poppy seeds
⅔ cup milk
1 egg, beaten lightly

1 Lightly grease a cookie sheet with a little butter.

2 Strain the self-raising flour and the all-purpose flour into a mixing bowl with the baking powder, salt, cayenne, curry powder, and poppy seeds.

3 Rub in the butter with your fingertips until the mixture resembles bread crumbs.

4 Add the milk and beaten egg and bring together with your fingers to form a soft dough.

5 Turn the dough out onto a lightly floured counter, then knead lightly for a few minutes.

6 Shape the dough into a circle about 2 inches/5 cm deep and mark a cross shape on the top with a sharp knife.

7 Bake in a preheated oven, 375°F/190°C, for 45 minutes.

8 Remove the bread from the oven, transfer to a wire rack, and let cool. Serve the bread cut into chunks or slices.

COOK'S TIP

If the bread looks as though it is browning too much, cover it with foil for the remainder of the cooking time.

cheese & ham loaf

makes one loaf

6 tbsp butter, diced, plus extra
    for greasing
generous 1½ cups self-rising flour
1 tsp salt
2 tsp baking powder
1 tsp paprika
1¼ cups grated sharp cheese
scant ½ cup chopped smoked ham
2 eggs, beaten lightly
⅔ cup milk

COOK'S TIP

This tasty bread is best eaten on
the day it is made, as it does not
keep for very long.

1 Grease a 1-lb/450-g loaf pan
   with a little butter and line the
base with baking parchment.

2 Strain the flour, salt, baking
   powder, and paprika into a large
mixing bowl.

3 Rub in the butter with your
   fingertips until the mixture
resembles fine bread crumbs. Stir
in the cheese and ham.

4 Add the beaten eggs and milk
   to the dry ingredients in the
bowl and mix well.

5 Spoon the cheese and ham
   mixture into the prepared pan.

6 Bake in a preheated oven,
   350°F/180°C, for about 1 hour,
or until the loaf is well risen.

7 Let the bread cool in the pan,
   then turn out, and transfer to
a wire rack to cool completely.

8 Cut the bread into thick slices
   to serve.

sun-dried tomato rolls

makes eight

⅓ cup butter, melted and cooled
   slightly, plus extra for greasing
generous 1½ cups strong white
   bread flour, plus extra
   for dusting
½ tsp salt
1 envelope active dry yeast
3 tbsp lukewarm milk
2 eggs, beaten lightly
1¾ oz/50 g sun-dried tomatoes in
   oil, drained and finely chopped
milk, for brushing

VARIATION
Add some finely chopped
anchovies or olives to the dough
in step 5 for extra flavor,
if you wish.

---

1 Lightly grease a cookie sheet
   with a little butter.

2 Strain the flour and salt into a
   large mixing bowl. Stir in the dry
yeast, then pour in the melted butter,
milk, and eggs. Bring together to form
a dough.

3 Turn the dough out onto a
   lightly floured counter and knead
for about 5 minutes, until smooth.
Alternatively, use an electric mixer with
a dough hook.

4 Place the dough in a greased
   bowl, cover, and let rise in a
warm place for 1–1½ hours, or until
the dough has doubled in size.

5 Punch down the dough for
   2–3 minutes. Knead the sun-dried
tomatoes into the dough, sprinkling
the counter with extra flour, because
the tomatoes are quite oily.

6 Divide the dough into 8 even-size
   balls and place them on the
prepared cookie sheet. Cover and let
rise for about 30 minutes, or until the
rolls have doubled in size.

7 Brush the rolls with milk and
   bake in a preheated oven,
450°F/230°C, for 10–15 minutes,
or until they are golden brown.

8 Transfer the tomato rolls to a
   wire rack and let cool slightly
before serving.

garlic bread rolls

makes eight

1 tbsp butter, for greasing

12 garlic cloves

1½ cups milk, plus extra
    for brushing

3½ cups strong white bread flour,
    plus extra for dusting

1 tsp salt

1 envelope active dry yeast

1 tbsp dried mixed herbs

2 tbsp sunflower oil

1 egg, beaten lightly

rock salt, for sprinkling

1 Lightly grease a cookie sheet with the butter.

2 Peel the garlic cloves and place them in a pan with the milk. Bring to a boil over low heat and simmer gently for 15 minutes. Let cool slightly, then place in a blender or food processor, and process into a paste.

3 Strain the flour and salt into a large mixing bowl and stir in the dry yeast and mixed herbs.

4 Add the garlic-flavored milk, sunflower oil, and beaten egg to the dry ingredients, mix well, and bring together with your fingers to form a dough.

5 Turn the dough out onto a lightly floured counter and knead lightly for a few minutes until smooth and soft.

6 Place the dough in a greased bowl, cover, and let rise in a warm place for about 1 hour, or until doubled in size.

7 Punch down the dough for 2 minutes. Divide into 8, shape into rolls, and place on the cookie sheet. Score the top of each roll with a knife, cover, and leave for 15 minutes.

8 Brush the rolls with milk and sprinkle rock salt over the top.

9 Bake in a preheated oven, 425°F/220°C, for 15–20 minutes. Transfer the rolls to a wire rack to cool before serving.

mini focaccia

serves four

2 tbsp olive oil, plus extra
  for brushing

2½ cups strong white bread flour,
  plus extra for dusting

½ tsp salt

1 envelope active dry yeast

1 cup lukewarm water

1 cup pitted green or black olives,
  cut in half

TOPPING

2 red onions, sliced

2 tbsp olive oil

1 tsp sea salt

1 tbsp fresh thyme leaves

1 Lightly brush several cookie
  sheets with olive oil. Strain the
flour and salt into a large bowl, then
stir in the yeast. Pour in the olive oil
and water and bring together with
your fingers to form a dough.

2 Turn the dough out onto a lightly
  floured counter and knead for
about 5 minutes. Alternatively, use an
electric mixer with a dough hook and
knead for 7–8 minutes.

3 Place the dough in a greased
  bowl, cover, and let stand in a
warm place for about 1–1½ hours, or
until it has doubled in size.

4 Punch down the dough for
  1–2 minutes. Knead half of the
olives into the dough. Divide the
dough into fourths and then shape the
fourths into circles. Place them on the
cookie sheets and push your fingers
into them to achieve a dimpled effect.

5 To make the topping, sprinkle the
  red onions and remaining olives
over the dough circles. Drizzle the olive
oil over the top of the onions and
olives, then sprinkle with the sea salt
and thyme leaves. Cover and let rise
for 30 minutes.

6 Bake in a preheated oven,
  375°F/190°C, for 20–25 minutes,
or until the focaccia are golden.

7 Transfer to a wire rack and let
  cool before serving.

VARIATION
Use this quantity of dough
to make 1 large focaccia,
if you like.

soda bread

1 tbsp butter, for greasing

generous 2 cups all-purpose flour,
 plus extra for dusting

generous 2 cups whole-wheat flour

2 tsp baking powder

1 tsp baking soda

2 tbsp superfine sugar

1 tsp salt

1 egg, beaten lightly

generous 1¾ cups plain yogurt

VARIATION

For a fruity version of this soda bread, add ¾ cup of raisins to the dry ingredients in step 2.

---

1 Grease a cookie sheet with the butter and dust lightly with flour.

2 Strain both types of flour, the baking powder, baking soda, sugar, and salt into a large bowl, and add any bran remaining in the strainer.

3 In a pitcher, beat together the egg and yogurt and pour the mixture into the dry ingredients. Mix well, bringing together to form a soft and sticky dough.

4 Knead the dough for a few minutes on a lightly floured counter until smooth, then shape it into a large round about 2 inches/ 5 cm deep.

5 Transfer the dough to the prepared cookie sheet. Mark a cross shape on top with a sharp knife.

6 Bake in a preheated oven, 375°F/190°C, for 40 minutes, or until the bread is golden brown.

7 Transfer the loaf to a wire rack and let cool completely. Cut into slices to serve.

Cookies

Nothing can compare with a homemade cookie for bringing a touch of pleasure to a coffee break or tea-time. This selection of delicious cookies and after-dinner treats will tantalize your taste buds and keep you coming back for more.

Tempting cookies, such as Citrus Crescents, Meringues, Rock Drops, and Gingersnaps, are quick, easy, and satisfying to make. You can easily vary the ingredients to suit your taste—the possibilities for inventiveness when making cookies are endless and this chapter shows you how.

savory curried crackers

makes forty

scant ½ cup butter, softened, plus extra for greasing

¾ cup all-purpose flour, plus extra for dusting

1 tsp salt

2 tsp curry powder

1 cup grated mellow semihard cheese

1 cup freshly grated Parmesan cheese

COOK'S TIP

These crackers can be stored for several days in an airtight container.

1 Lightly grease about 4 cookie sheets with a little butter.

2 Strain the flour and salt into a mixing bowl.

3 Stir in the curry powder and both the grated cheeses. Rub in the softened butter with your fingertips, then bring the mixture together to form a soft dough.

4 Roll out the dough thinly on a lightly floured counter to form a rectangle.

5 Cut out 40 crackers using a 2-inch/5-cm cookie cutter.

6 Arrange the crackers on the cookie sheets.

7 Bake in a preheated oven, 350°F/180°C, for 10–15 minutes, until golden brown.

8 Let the crackers cool slightly on the cookie sheets. Transfer them to a wire rack to cool completely and crispen, then serve.

3

4

5

rosemary cookies

makes twenty-five

1¾ oz/50g butter, softened, plus
    extra for greasing

1¾ oz/50g superfine sugar

grated rind of 1 lemon

4 tbsp lemon juice

1 egg, separated

2 tsp finely chopped fresh rosemary

scant 1½ cups all-purpose flour,
    strained, plus extra for dusting

superfine sugar,
    for sprinkling

VARIATION

In place of the fresh rosemary,
use 1½ teaspoons of dried
rosemary, if you like.

1 Lightly grease 2 cookie sheets
with a little butter.

2 Cream the butter and sugar
together in a large mixing bowl
until pale and fluffy.

3 Add the lemon rind and juice,
then the egg yolk, and beat until
the mixture is thoroughly blended. Stir
in the chopped fresh rosemary.

4 Mix in the strained flour and
bring together with your fingers
to form a soft dough. Wrap in plastic
wrap and place in the refrigerator to
chill for 30 minutes.

5 Roll out the dough thinly on a
lightly floured counter. Stamp out
about 25 circles with a 2½-inch/6-cm
cookie cutter. Arrange the dough circles
on the prepared cookie sheets.

6 Lightly whisk the egg white
in a small bowl. Gently brush
the egg white over the surface of each
cookie, then sprinkle with a little
superfine sugar.

7 Bake in a preheated oven,
350°F/180°C, for 15 minutes.

8 Transfer the cookies to a wire rack
and let cool before serving.

cheese sablés

makes thirty-five

⅔ cup butter, diced, plus extra
    for greasing
generous 1 cup all-purpose flour,
    plus extra for dusting
1½ cups grated sharp cheese
1 egg yolk
sesame seeds, for sprinkling

COOK'S TIP
Cut out any shape you like
for your savory sablés. Children
will enjoy them cut into animal
shapes or other fun designs.

1 Lightly grease several cookie
  sheets with a little butter.

2 Combine the flour and grated
  cheese in a bowl.

3 Add the butter to the cheese
  and flour mixture and rub in
with your fingertips until the mixture
resembles bread crumbs.

4 Stir in the egg yolk. Bring together
  to form a dough. Wrap in plastic
wrap and chill for 30 minutes.

5 Roll out the cheese dough thinly
  on a lightly floured counter.
Stamp out circles with a 2½-inch/6-cm
cookie cutter, re-rolling the trimmings
to make about 35 crackers.

6 Carefully transfer the dough
  circles onto the prepared cookie
sheets and sprinkle the sesame seeds
evenly over the top of them.

7 Bake in a preheated oven,
  200°C/400°F, for 20 minutes,
until lightly golden.

8 Carefully transfer the cheese
  sablés to a wire rack and let cool
slightly before serving.

VARIATION
For a sweet variation of these
traditional French cookies,
substitute the grated rind of
1 lemon for the cheese and stir in
125 g/4½ oz superfine sugar at
the end of step 2. Beat the egg
yolk with 1 tablespoon brandy
before adding it to the mixture.
Roll out the dough, stamp out
circles, and bake as above.

cheese & chive biscuits

makes ten

generous 1½ cups self-rising flour,
plus extra for dusting

1 tsp mustard powder

½ tsp cayenne pepper

½ tsp salt

½ cup lowfat soft cheese with
added herbs

2 tbsp chopped fresh chives, plus
extra to garnish

scant ½ cup skim milk, plus 2 tbsp
for brushing

generous ½ cup grated reduced-fat
sharp colby cheese

lowfat soft cheese, to serve

1 Strain the flour, mustard, cayenne,
and salt into a mixing bowl.

2 Add the soft cheese to the
flour mixture and stir together
until well blended, then stir in the
chopped chives.

3 Make a well in the center of the
ingredients and gradually pour in
the skim milk, stirring as you pour,
bringing together with your fingers to
form a soft dough.

4 Turn the dough out onto a floured
counter and knead lightly. Roll
out to a thickness of ¾ inch/2 cm.
Stamp out as many circles as you can
using a 2-inch/5-cm plain cookie cutter.
Transfer the circles to a cookie sheet.

5 Knead the dough trimmings
together and roll out again.
Stamp out more circles—you should
be able to make 10 biscuits in total.

6 Brush the biscuits with the
remaining milk and sprinkle
with the grated cheese. Bake in a
preheated oven, 400°F/200°C, for
15–20 minutes, until risen and golden.
Transfer to a wire rack to cool. Serve
warm with lowfat soft cheese,
garnished with chopped chives.

cheese & mustard biscuits

makes eight

4 tbsp butter, diced, plus extra
      for greasing
generous 1½ cups self-rising flour,
      plus extra for dusting
1 tsp baking powder
pinch of salt
1¼ cups grated sharp cheese
1 tsp mustard powder
⅔ cup milk, plus extra for brushing
pepper

1 Lightly grease a cookie sheet with a little butter.

2 Strain the flour, baking powder, and salt into a mixing bowl. Rub in the butter with your fingertips until the mixture resembles bread crumbs.

3 Stir in the grated cheese, mustard powder, and enough milk to form a soft dough.

4 Knead the dough very lightly on a lightly floured counter. Flatten it out with the palm of your hand to a depth of about 1 inch/2.5 cm.

5 Cut the dough into 8 wedges with a knife. Brush the wedges with a little milk and sprinkle with pepper to taste.

6 Bake in a preheated oven, 425°F/220°C, for 10–15 minutes, until the biscuits are golden brown.

7 Transfer the biscuits to a wire rack and let cool slightly before serving.

gingersnaps

makes thirty

½ cup butter, plus extra for greasing

2½ cups self-rising flour

pinch of salt

1 cup superfine sugar

1 tbsp ground ginger

1 tsp baking soda

¼ cup light corn syrup

1 egg, beaten lightly

1 tsp grated orange rind

COOK'S TIP

Store these cookies in an airtight container and eat them within 1 week.

VARIATION

For less traditional, but equally delicious cookies , substitute 1 tablespoon apple pie spice for the ground ginger and 1 teaspoon finely grated lemon rind for the orange rind.

1 Lightly grease several cookie sheets with a little butter.

2 Strain the flour, salt, sugar, ground ginger, and baking soda into a large mixing bowl.

3 Put the butter and light corn syrup into a pan and place the pan over very low heat until the butter has melted.

4 Remove the pan from the heat and let the butter mixture cool slightly, then pour the mixture onto the dry ingredients.

5 Add the egg and orange rind and bring together to form a dough.

6 Using your hands, carefully shape the dough into 30 even-size balls.

7 Place the balls well apart on the prepared cookie sheets, then flatten them slightly with your fingers.

8 Bake in a preheated oven, 325°F/160°C, for 15–20 minutes. Transfer the cookies to a wire rack to cool and crispen before serving.

lemon jumbles

makes fifty

⅓ cup butter, softened, plus extra
   for greasing
generous ½ cup superfine sugar
grated rind of 1 lemon
1 egg, beaten lightly
4 tbsp lemon juice
2½ cups all-purpose flour, plus extra
   for dusting
1 tsp baking powder
1 tbsp milk
confectioners' sugar, for dredging

VARIATION

If you prefer, form the dough into other shapes—letters of the alphabet or geometric designs.

---

1 Lightly grease several cookie sheets with a little butter.

2 Cream the butter, superfine sugar, and lemon rind together in a mixing bowl until pale and fluffy.

3 Add the beaten egg and lemon juice, a little at a time, beating thoroughly after each addition.

4 Strain the flour and baking powder into the mixture and mix until blended. Add the milk and bring together with your fingers to form a soft dough.

5 Turn the dough out onto a lightly floured counter and divide into about 50 equal-size pieces.

6 Roll each piece into a sausage shape with your hands and bend into an "S" shape.

7 Place the dough shapes on the prepared cookie sheets and bake in a preheated oven, 325°F/160°C, for 15–20 minutes. Transfer to a wire rack and let cool completely. Dredge generously with confectioners' sugar before serving.

cinnamon & seed squares

makes twelve

generous 1 cup butter, softened,
  plus extra for greasing

1¼ cups superfine sugar

3 eggs, beaten lightly

1¾ cups self-rising flour

½ tsp baking soda

1 tbsp ground cinnamon

⅔ cup sour cream

3½ oz/100 g sunflower seeds

COOK'S TIP

These moist squares will
freeze well and will keep for
up to 1 month.

---

1 Grease a 9-inch/23-cm square
cake pan with a little butter and
line the base with baking parchment.

2 Cream together the butter and
superfine sugar in a large
mixing bowl until the mixture is light
and fluffy.

3 Gradually add the beaten eggs to
the mixture, beating thoroughly
after each addition.

4 Strain the self-rising flour, baking
soda, and ground cinnamon
into the creamed mixture, then fold
in gently, using a metal spoon in a
figure-eight movement.

5 Spoon in the sour cream and
sunflower seeds and mix gently
until well blended.

6 Spoon the cake batter into the
prepared cake pan, then level
the surface with the back of a spoon
or a spatula.

7 Bake in a preheated oven,
350°F/180°C, for 45 minutes,
until the surface is firm to the touch
when pressed with a finger.

8 Loosen the edges with a round-
bladed knife, then turn out onto a
wire rack to cool completely. Slice into
12 squares before serving.

oat & raisin cookies

makes ten

4 tbsp butter, plus extra for greasing

generous ½ cup superfine sugar

1 egg, lightly beaten

generous ⅓ cup all-purpose flour

½ tsp salt

½ tsp baking powder

2 cups rolled oats

¾ cup raisins

2 tbsp sesame seeds

COOK'S TIP

To enjoy these cookies at
their best, store them in an
airtight container.

1 Lightly grease 2 cookie sheets with a little butter.

2 Cream the butter and sugar together in a large mixing bowl until light and fluffy.

3 Gradually add the beaten egg, beating well after each addition until thoroughly blended.

4 Strain the flour, salt, and baking powder into the creamed mixture. Mix together gently. Add the oats, raisins, and sesame seeds, and mix together thoroughly.

5 Place 10 spoonfuls of the mixture on the prepared cookie sheets, spaced well apart to allow room to expand during cooking, and flatten them slightly with the back of a spoon.

6 Bake in a preheated oven, 350°F/180°C, for 15 minutes.

7 Let the cookies cool slightly on the cookie sheets.

8 Carefully transfer the cookies to a wire rack and let cool completely before serving.

hazelnut squares

makes sixteen

⅓ cup butter, diced, plus extra
    for greasing
generous 1 cup all-purpose flour
pinch of salt
1 tsp baking powder
¾ cup brown sugar
1 egg, beaten lightly
4 tbsp milk
1 cup hazelnuts, cut into halves
raw brown sugar, for
    sprinkling (optional)

1 Grease a 9-inch/23-cm square cake pan with a little butter and line the base with baking parchment.

2 Strain the flour, salt, and the baking powder into a large mixing bowl.

3 Rub in the butter with your fingertips until the mixture resembles fine bread crumbs. Add the brown sugar to the mixture and stir to blend.

4 Add the beaten egg, milk, and nuts to the mixture and stir well until thoroughly blended and the mixture has a soft consistency.

5 Spoon the mixture into the prepared cake pan and level the surface with a spatula. Sprinkle with raw brown sugar, if you like.

VARIATION

For a coffee time cookie, replace the milk with the same amount of cold strong black coffee—the stronger the better.

6 Bake in a preheated oven, 350°F/ 180°C, for 25 minutes, or until the surface is firm to the touch when pressed with a finger.

7 Let cool in the pan for about 10 minutes, then loosen the edges with a round-bladed knife, and turn out onto a wire rack. Cut into 16 squares to serve.

rock drops

makes eight

⅓ cup butter, diced, plus extra
for greasing

scant 1½ cups all-purpose flour

2 tsp baking powder

⅓ cup raw brown sugar

½ cup golden raisins

2 tbsp candied cherries,
chopped finely

1 egg, beaten lightly

2 tbsp milk

COOK'S TIP

For convenience, prepare the dry
ingredients in advance and just
before cooking, stir in the liquid.

1 Lightly grease a cookie sheet
with a little butter.

2 Strain the flour and baking
powder into a mixing bowl. Rub
in the butter with your fingertips until
the mixture resembles bread crumbs.

3 Stir in the raw brown sugar,
raisins, and candied cherries.

4 Add the beaten egg and milk to
the mixture and bring together to
form a soft dough.

5 Spoon 8 mounds of the mixture
onto the prepared cookie sheet,
spacing them well apart to allow room
to expand during cooking.

6 Bake in a preheated oven,
400°F/200°C, for 15–20 minutes,
until firm to the touch when pressed
with a finger.

7 Remove the rock drops from the
cookie sheet. Serve piping hot
from the oven, or transfer to a wire
rack and let cool before serving.

coconut flapjacks

makes sixteen

1 cup butter, plus extra
  for greasing
1 cup raw brown sugar
2 tbsp light corn syrup
3½ cups rolled oats
1 cup dry unsweetened coconut
⅓ cup chopped candied cherries

COOK'S TIP

The flapjacks are best stored in
an airtight container and eaten
within 1 week. They can also be
frozen for up to 1 month.

VARIATION

For plain flapjacks, heat
3 tablespoons superfine sugar,
3 tablespoons light corn syrup,
and ½ cup butter in a pan over
low heat until the butter has
melted. Stir in 1¾ cups rolled
oats or oat flakes until combined,
then transfer to a greased cookie
sheet, and bake as above.

1 Lightly grease a 12 x 9-inch/
30 x 23-cm cookie sheet with
a little butter.

2 Heat the butter, raw brown sugar,
and light corn syrup in a large
pan over low heat until just melted.

3 Stir in the oats, shredded coconut,
and candied cherries and mix well
until evenly combined.

4 Place the mixture on the prepared
cookie sheet. Spread evenly
across the cookie sheet and level the
surface by pressing with a spatula.

5 Bake the flapjack in a preheated
oven, 325°F/170°C, for about
30 minutes, until golden.

6 Remove from the oven and
let cool on the cookie sheet for
10 minutes.

7 Cut the mixture into 16 pieces
using a sharp knife.

8 Carefully transfer the flapjack
squares to a wire rack and let
cool completely.

citrus crescents

makes twenty-five

⅓ cup butter, softened, plus extra
   for greasing
⅓ cup superfine sugar, plus extra
   for dusting (optional)
1 egg, separated
scant 1½ cups all-purpose flour, plus
   extra for dusting
grated rind of 1 orange
grated rind of 1 lemon
grated rind of 1 lime
2–3 tbsp orange juice

1 Lightly grease 2 cookie sheets with a little butter.

2 Cream the butter and sugar together in a mixing bowl until light and fluffy, then gradually beat in the egg yolk.

3 Strain the flour into the creamed mixture and mix until evenly blended. Add the orange, lemon, and lime rinds to the mixture, with enough orange juice to form a soft dough.

4 Roll out the dough on a lightly floured counter. Stamp out circles using a 3-inch/7.5-cm cookie cutter. Make crescent shapes by cutting away a fourth of each circle. Re-roll the trimmings to make about 25 crescents.

5 Place the crescents on the prepared cookie sheets. Prick the surface of each crescent with a fork.

6 Lightly whisk the egg white in a small bowl and brush it over the cookies. Dust with extra superfine sugar, if you like.

7 Bake in a preheated oven, 400°F/200°C, for 12–15 minutes. Transfer the cookies to a wire rack to cool and crispen before serving.

spiced cookies

makes twelve

¾ cup sweet butter, plus extra

    for greasing

scant 1 cup dark brown sugar

generous 1½ cups all-purpose flour

pinch of salt

½ tsp baking soda

1 tsp ground cinnamon

½ tsp ground coriander

½ tsp ground nutmeg

¼ tsp ground cloves

2 tbsp dark rum

1 Lightly grease 2 cookie sheets with a little butter.

2 Cream the butter and sugar together in a mixing bowl and whisk until light and fluffy.

3 Strain the flour, salt and baking soda into the butter and sugar mixture, then stir in the cinnamon, coriander, nutmeg, and cloves.

4 Add the dark rum and stir it into the creamed mixture.

5 Place small mounds of the mixture on the prepared cookie sheets using 2 teaspoons. Space the mounds well apart to allow room to expand during cooking. Flatten each one slightly with the back of a spoon.

6 Bake in a preheated oven at 350°F/180°C for 10–12 minutes, until golden brown in color.

7 Carefully transfer the cookies to wire racks to cool completely and crispen before serving.

COOK'S TIP
Use the back of a fork to flatten the cookies instead of a spoon, to give them a textured surface.

peanut butter cookies

makes twenty

½ cup butter, softened, plus extra
   for greasing
½ cup chunky peanut butter
generous 1 cup granulated sugar
1 egg, beaten lightly
generous 1 cup all-purpose flour
½ tsp baking powder
pinch of salt
½ cup chopped unsalted
   natural peanuts

COOK'S TIP
For a crunchy bite and
sparkling appearance, sprinkle
the cookies with raw brown
sugar before baking.

VARIATION
For a change, use light molasses
sugar instead of granulated and
add 1 teaspoon apple pie
spice with the flour and
baking powder.

1 Lightly grease 2 cookie sheets.
with a little butter.

2 Beat the softened butter and
peanut butter together in a large
mixing bowl.

3 Gradually add the granulated
sugar and beat well.

4 Add the beaten egg, a little at a
time, beating after each addition
until thoroughly blended.

5 Strain the flour, baking powder,
and salt into the creamed peanut
butter mixture.

6 Add the chopped peanuts
and bring the mixture together
with your fingers to form a soft, sticky
dough. Wrap the cookie dough in
plastic wrap and chill in the refrigerator
for 30 minutes.

7 Form the dough into 20 balls
and place them on the prepared
cookie sheets, spaced well apart to
allow room to expand during cooking,
and flatten slightly with your hand.

8 Bake in a preheated oven,
375°F/190°C, for 15 minutes,
until golden brown. Transfer the
cookies to a wire rack and let cool
before serving.

shortbread fantails

makes eight

½ cup butter, softened, plus extra
for greasing
scant ¼ cup granulated sugar
2 tbsp confectioners' sugar
generous 1½ cups all-purpose flour,
plus extra for dusting
pinch of salt
2 tsp orange flower water
superfine sugar, for sprinkling

1 Grease a shallow 8-inch/20-cm
round cake pan with butter.

2 Cream the butter, granulated
sugar, and confectioners'
sugar together in a large mixing bowl until
light and fluffy.

3 Strain the flour and salt into the
creamed mixture. Add the orange
flower water and bring together with
your fingers to form a soft dough.

4 Roll out the dough on a lightly
floured counter into an 8-inch/
20-cm circle and place in the prepared
pan. Prick well and score into
8 triangles with a round-bladed knife.

5 Bake the shortbread in a
preheated oven, 325°F/160°C, for
30–35 minutes, or until it is crisp and
the top is pale golden.

6 Sprinkle with superfine sugar,
then cut along the marked lines
to make the fantails.

7 Let the shortbread cool in the pan
before serving.

meringues

makes thirteen

4 egg whites
pinch of salt
generous ½ cup granulated sugar
generous ½ cup superfine sugar
1¼ cups heavy cream,
    whipped lightly

VARIATION

For a finer texture, replace
the granulated sugar with
superfine sugar.

---

1 Line 3 large cookie sheets with baking parchment.

2 Whisk the egg whites and salt in a large clean bowl until stiff, using an electric whisk or a balloon whisk. (You should be able to turn the bowl upside down without any movement from the egg whites.)

3 Whisk in the granulated sugar, a little at a time; the meringue should start to look glossy.

4 Whisk in the superfine sugar, a little at a time, whisking well after each addition until all the sugar has been incorporated and the meringue is thick, white, and forms peaks.

5 Transfer the meringue mixture into a pastry bag fitted with a ¾-inch/2-cm star tip. Pipe about 26 small whirls of meringue onto the prepared cookie sheets.

6 Bake in a preheated oven, 250°F/120°C, for 1½ hours, or until the meringues are pale golden and can be easily lifted off the parchment. Turn off the heat and let cool in the oven overnight.

7 Just before serving, sandwich the meringue whirls together in pairs with the whipped cream and arrange on a serving plate.

vanilla hearts

makes twelve

⅔ cup butter, diced, plus extra
    for greasing

2 cups all-purpose flour, plus extra
    for dusting

½ cup superfine sugar, plus extra
    for dusting

1 tsp vanilla extract

COOK'S TIP

Place a fresh vanilla bean in
your superfine sugar and keep
it in a storage jar for several
weeks to give the sugar a
delicious vanilla flavor.

VARIATION

If you like, you could add a few
drops of red or pink food
coloring with the vanilla
extract and decorate the the
hearts with tiny silver, gold, or
pink balls.

1 Lightly grease a cookie sheet
with a little butter.

2 Strain the flour into a large mixing
bowl and rub in the butter with
your fingertips until the mixture
resembles fine bread crumbs.

3 Stir in the superfine sugar and
vanilla extract and bring the
mixture together with your hands
to form a firm dough.

4 Roll out the dough on a lightly
floured surface to a thickness of
1 inch/2.5 cm. Stamp out 12 hearts
with a heart-shaped cookie cutter
measuring about 2 inches/5 cm
across and 1 inch/2.5 cm deep.

5 Arrange the hearts on the
prepared cookie sheet. Bake in
a preheated oven, 350°F/180°C, for
15–20 minutes, until light golden.

6 Transfer the vanilla hearts to a
wire rack and let cool completely.
Dust the cookies with a little superfine
sugar just before serving.

Appetizers & Snacks

With so many fresh ingredients readily available, it is very easy to create some deliciously different appetizers to make the perfect introduction to any meal. The ideas in this chapter are an inspiration to cook and a treat to eat, and they give an edge to the appetite that makes the main course even more enjoyable. When choosing an appetizer, make sure that you provide a good balance of flavors, colors, and textures that offer variety and contrast. Balance the nature of the recipes too—a rich entrée is best preceded by a light appetizer to stimulate the taste buds.

onion & mozzarella tarts

serves four

9 oz/250 g puff pastry dough,
   thawed if frozen

2 red onions

1 red bell pepper

8 cherry tomatoes, halved

3½ oz/100 g mozzarella cheese,
   cut into chunks

8 fresh thyme sprigs

1 Roll out the pie dough on a
lightly floured counter to make
4 squares, 3 inches/7.5 cm wide. Trim
the edges of the dough, reserving the
trimmings. Chill the dough in the
refrigerator for 30 minutes.

2 Place the dough squares on a
cookie sheet. Brush a little water
around the edges of each square and
use the reserved dough trimmings to
make a rim around each tart.

3 Cut the red onions into thin
wedges and halve and seed the
red bell pepper.

4 Place the onions and red bell
pepper on a broiler rack. Cook
under a preheated medium broiler for
15 minutes, or until the bell pepper
skin is charred.

5 Place the roasted bell pepper
halves in a plastic bag and set
aside to sweat for 10 minutes. When
the bell pepper is cool enough to
handle, peel off the skin and cut the
flesh into strips.

6 Line the dough squares with
squares of foil. Bake in a
preheated oven, 400°F/200°C, for
10 minutes. Remove and discard the
foil, then bake the pastry squares for
5 minutes more.

7 Divide the onions, bell pepper
strips, tomatoes, and cheese
among the tarts and sprinkle with
the fresh thyme.

8 Bake the tarts for 15 minutes
more, or until they are golden.
Transfer to warmed serving plates if
serving hot, or to a wire rack to cool if
serving cold.

baked eggplant

serves four

3–4 tbsp olive oil

2 garlic cloves, crushed

2 large eggplant

3½ oz/100 g mozzarella cheese

generous ¾ cup bottled
     strained tomatoes

scant ⅔ cup freshly grated
     Parmesan cheese

1 Heat 2 tablespoons of the olive oil in a large skillet. Add the garlic and sauté over a low heat for 30 seconds.

2 Slice the eggplant lengthwise. Add the slices to the skillet and cook in the oil for 3–4 minutes on each side, or until tender (you may have to do this in batches, so add the remaining oil as necessary.)

3 Remove the eggplant with a slotted spoon and drain on paper towels.

4 Place a layer of eggplant slices in a shallow ovenproof dish. Thinly slice the mozzarella, then place a layer of cheese slices over the eggplant. Pour over a third of the tomatoes. Continue layering in the same order, finishing with a layer of tomatoes.

5 Generously sprinkle the grated Parmesan cheese over the top of the dish. Bake in a preheated oven, 400°F/200°C, for 25–30 minutes, or until the top is golden and bubbling.

6 Transfer the baked eggplant to serving plates and serve warm, or let cool, then chill and serve cold.

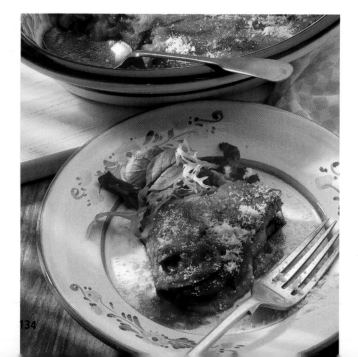

baked fennel

serves four

2 fennel bulbs

2 celery stalks, cut into 3-inch/
    7.5-cm pieces

6 sun-dried tomatoes, cut in half

generous ¾ cup bottled
    strained tomatoes

2 tsp dried oregano

scant ⅔ cup freshly grated
    Parmesan cheese

1 Trim the fennel using a sharp knife, discard any tough outer leaves, and cut the bulbs into fourths.

2 Bring a large pan of water to a boil, add the fennel and celery, and cook for 8–10 minutes, or until just tender. Remove with a slotted spoon and drain.

3 Place the fennel pieces, celery, and sun-dried tomatoes in a large ovenproof dish.

4 Mix the tomatoes and oregano in a bowl and pour the mixture over the vegetables in the dish.

5 Sprinkle with the Parmesan cheese and bake in a preheated oven, 375°F/190°C, for 20 minutes, or until hot. Serve as an appetizer or as a vegetable side dish.

cheese & onion pies

FILLING

3 tbsp vegetable oil

4 onions, thinly sliced

4 garlic cloves, crushed

4 tbsp finely chopped fresh parsley

¾ cup grated sharp cheese

salt and pepper

DOUGH

1¼ cups all-purpose flour, plus extra
   for dusting

½ tsp salt

⅓ cup butter, diced

3–4 tbsp water

COOK'S TIP

You can prepare the filling in
advance and store it in the
refrigerator until required.

VARIATION

Use red or white onions for an
extra sweet, mild flavor and
sprinkle with 1 teaspoon of sugar
5 minutes before the end of the
cooking time in step 1.

---

1 Heat the oil in a skillet over low
heat. Add the onions and garlic
and cook for 10–15 minutes, or until
the onions are soft. Remove the skillet
from the heat, stir in the parsley and
cheese, and season to taste.

2 To make the dough, strain the
flour and salt into a bowl. Rub in
the butter with your fingertips until the
mixture resembles bread crumbs.
Gradually stir in the water and bring
together to form a dough.

3 Roll out the dough on a lightly
floured counter and divide it into
8 portions.

4 Roll out each portion into a circle
4 inches/10 cm wide and use 4 of
the circles to line individual tartlet
pans. Fill each pie shell with a fourth
of the cheese and onion mixture.

5 Cover the pies with the remaining
4 dough circles. Make a slit in
the top of each pie with the point of a
sharp knife to allow steam to escape
during cooking, then press the edges
of the pies firmly with the back of a
teaspoon to seal.

6 Bake in a preheated oven,
425°F/220°C, for 20 minutes.
Transfer the cheese and onion pies to
warmed plates and serve.

stuffed tomato

serves six

6 large, firm tomatoes, rinsed

4 tbsp sweet butter

5 tbsp vegetable oil

1 onion, chopped finely

1 tsp finely chopped fresh
   gingerroot

1 tsp crushed garlic

1 tsp pepper

1 tsp salt

½ tsp garam masala

4 cups ground lamb

1 fresh green chile, seeded and
   finely chopped

fresh cilantro leaves

1 Slice the tops off the tomatoes and reserve, then scoop out the pulp. Grease an ovenproof dish with all of the butter and place the tomatoes in the dish.

2 Heat the oil in a pan over medium heat, add the onion, and cook, stirring frequently, until golden.

3 Reduce the heat and add the ginger, garlic, pepper, salt, and garam masala. Cook for 3–5 minutes.

4 Add the ground lamb and cook for 15 minutes, until browned.

5 Add the green chile and fresh cilantro leaves and cook for 3–5 minutes more.

6 Spoon the lamb mixture into the tomatoes and replace the tops. Bake in a preheated oven, 350°F/ 180°C, for 15–20 minutes.

7 Transfer the tomatoes to serving plates and serve hot.

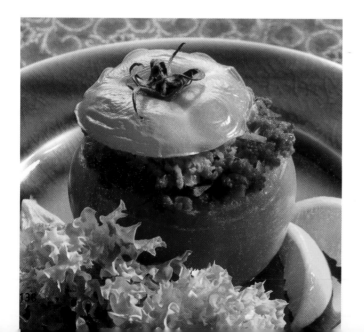

pasta-stuffed tomatoes

serves eight

5 tbsp extra virgin olive oil, plus
    extra for greasing

8 beefsteak tomatoes or large round
    tomatoes, rinsed

1 cup dried ditalini or other very
    small pasta shapes

8 black olives, pitted and
    finely chopped

2 tbsp finely chopped fresh basil

1 tbsp finely chopped fresh parsley

⅔ cup freshly grated
    Parmesan cheese

salt and pepper

fresh basil sprigs, to garnish

1 Brush a cookie sheet with olive oil. Slice the tops off the tomatoes and reserve to use as lids. If the tomatoes will not stand up, cut a thin slice off the base of each of them.

2 Scoop out the tomato pulp into a strainer using a teaspoon, and leave the pulp to drain. Invert the tomato shells on paper towels, pat dry, and let drain.

3 Bring a large pan of lightly salted water to a boil. Add the pasta and 1 tablespoon of the remaining olive oil, bring back to a boil, and cook for 8–10 minutes, or until tender but still firm to the bite. Drain and set aside.

4 Put the olives, basil, parsley, and Parmesan cheese into a large mixing bowl and stir in the drained tomato pulp. Add the pasta to the bowl. Stir in the remaining oil, mix together well, and season to taste.

5 Spoon the pasta mixture into the tomato shells and replace the lids. Arrange on the prepared cookie sheet and bake in a preheated oven, 375°F/190°C, for 15–20 minutes.

6 Remove the tomatoes from the oven and let cool until just warm.

7 Arrange the tomatoes on a serving dish, garnish with basil sprigs, and serve.

mexican-style pizzas

serves four

4 ready-made, pre-cooked
    individual pizza bases
1 tbsp olive oil
7 oz/200 g canned chopped
    tomatoes with garlic and herbs
2 tbsp tomato paste
7 oz/200 g canned kidney beans,
    drained and rinsed
⅔ cup corn kernels, thawed
    if frozen
1–2 tsp chili sauce
1 large red onion, shredded
1 cup grated sharp colby cheese
1 large fresh green chile, seeded
    and sliced into rings
salt and pepper

COOK'S TIP

Serve a Mexican-style salad
with this pizza. Arrange sliced
tomatoes, fresh cilantro leaves,
and a few slices of a small, ripe
avocado on a platter. Sprinkle
with fresh lime juice and
coarse sea salt.

1 Arrange the ready-made pizza bases on a large cookie sheet and brush the surfaces lightly with the olive oil.

2 Combine the chopped tomatoes, tomato paste, kidney beans, and corn in a large bowl and add chili sauce to taste. Season to taste with salt and pepper.

3 Spread the tomato and kidney bean mixture evenly over each of the pizza bases.

4 Top each pizza with shredded onion and sprinkle with some grated cheese and a few slices of fresh green chile to taste.

5 Bake in a preheated oven, 425°F/220°C, for 20 minutes, until the vegetables are tender, the cheese has melted, and the pizza dough is crisp and golden.

6 Remove the pizzas from the cookie sheet and transfer to serving plates. Serve hot.

mini pizzas

serves eight

BASIC PIZZA DOUGH

2 tsp dry yeast

1 tsp sugar

1 cup warm water

2½ cups strong white bread flour,
    plus extra for dusting

1 tsp salt

1 tbsp olive oil, plus extra
    for brushing

TOPPING

2 zucchini

generous ⅓ cup bottled
    strained tomatoes

½ cup diced pancetta

½ cup pitted black olives, chopped

1 tbsp mixed dried herbs

2 tbsp olive oil

salt and pepper

1 To make the dough, combine the yeast, sugar, and 4 tablespoons of the water. Set the mixture aside in a warm place for 15 minutes, until frothy.

2 In a separate bowl, combine the flour and salt and make a well in the center. Add the oil, yeast mixture, and remaining water. Mix into a smooth dough using a wooden spoon.

3 Turn the dough out onto a floured counter and knead for 4–5 minutes, or until smooth. Return the dough to the bowl, cover with an oiled sheet of plastic wrap, and let rise for 30 minutes, or until the dough has doubled in size.

4 Knead the dough for 2 minutes, then divide it into 8 balls. Roll out each portion thinly to form a circle about 4 inches/10 cm wide, then carefully transfer all of the dough circles to an oiled cookie sheet and push out the edges until the circles are even. The pizza doughs should be no more than ¼ inch/5 mm thick because they will rise during cooking.

5 To make the topping, grate the zucchini finely. Cover with paper towels and let stand for 10 minutes to soak up some of the juices.

6 Spread 2–3 teaspoons of the tomatoes over each pizza base and top with the grated zucchini, pancetta, and olives. Season with pepper, then add a sprinkling of mixed dried herbs to taste, and drizzle over the top with olive oil.

7 Bake in a preheated oven, 400°F/200°C, for 15 minutes, or until crispy. Season with salt and pepper to taste and serve hot.

creamy ham pizzas

serves four

9 oz/250 g flaky pastry dough,
    well chilled

3 tbsp butter

1 red onion, chopped

1 garlic clove, chopped

⅓ cup white bread flour

1¼ cups milk

scant ⅔ cup finely grated Parmesan
    cheese, plus extra for sprinkling

2 eggs, hard-cooked, cut
    into fourths

3½ oz/100 g Italian pork sausage,
    such as feline salame, cut
    into strips

salt and pepper

fresh thyme sprigs, to garnish

1 Fold the pastry dough in half and evenly grate it into 4 individual tart pans measuring 4 inches/10 cm wide. Using a floured fork, gently press the dough flakes down, making sure that there are no holes, and that the dough comes up the sides of the pans.

2 Line with foil and bake blind in a preheated oven, 425°F/220°C, for 10 minutes. Reduce the heat to 400°F/200°C, remove the foil from the pizza shells, and cook for 15 minutes, or until golden and set.

3 Heat the butter in a skillet. Add the onion and garlic and cook for 5–6 minutes, or until softened.

4 Add the flour, stirring well to coat the onion. Gradually stir in the milk to make a thick sauce.

5 Season the sauce with salt and pepper to taste and then stir in the Parmesan cheese. Do not reheat once the cheese has been added or the sauce will become too stringy.

6 Spread the sauce evenly over the cooked pizza shells. Decorate with the eggs and strips of sausage.

7 Sprinkle with a little extra Parmesan cheese, return to the oven, and bake for 5 minutes just to heat through.

8 Serve immediately, garnished with sprigs of fresh thyme.

gnocchi romana

serves four

scant 4 cups milk

pinch of freshly grated nutmeg

6 tbsp butter, plus extra
    for greasing

1¼ cups semolina

generous 1 cup freshly grated
    Parmesan cheese

2 eggs, beaten

½ cup grated Swiss cheese

salt and pepper

fresh basil sprigs, to garnish

1 Pour the milk into a pan and bring to a boil. Remove the pan from the heat and stir in the nutmeg and 2 tablespoons of the butter. Season to taste with salt and pepper.

2 Gradually stir the semolina into the milk, whisking to prevent lumps forming, then return to the stove over low heat. Simmer, stirring constantly, for about 10 minutes, or until very thick.

3 Beat ⅔ cup of the Parmesan cheese into the semolina mixture, then beat in the eggs. Continue beating the mixture until smooth. Let the mixture cool slightly.

4 Spread out the cooled semolina mixture in an even layer across a sheet of baking parchment, smoothing the surface with a damp spatula until it is about ½ inch/1 cm thick. Let cool completely, then chill the mixture in the refrigerator for 1 hour.

5 Remove the mixture from the refrigerator. Stamp out circles of gnocchi, about 1½ inches/4 cm wide, using a plain, greased cookie cutter.

6 Grease a shallow ovenproof dish or 4 individual ovenproof dishes. Lay the gnocchi trimmings in the base of the dish or dishes and arrange the circles of gnocchi on top, slightly overlapping each other.

7 Melt the remaining butter and drizzle it over the gnocchi. Sprinkle over the remaining grated Parmesan cheese, then sprinkle over the Swiss cheese.

8 Bake in a preheated oven, 400°F/200°C, for 25–30 minutes, until the top is crisp, golden brown, and bubbling. Serve immediately, garnished with fresh sprigs of basil.

spinach & ricotta shells

serves four

14 oz/400 g dried lumache rigate
   grande pasta

5 tbsp olive oil

1 cup fresh white bread crumbs

½ cup milk

10½ oz/300 g frozen spinach,
   thawed and drained

1 cup ricotta cheese

pinch of freshly grated nutmeg

14 oz/400 g canned chopped
   tomatoes, drained

1 garlic clove, crushed

salt and pepper

1 Bring a large pan of lightly salted water to a boil. Add the pasta and 1 tablespoon of the oil, bring back to a boil, and cook for 8–10 minutes, until just tender but still firm to the bite. Drain the pasta, refresh under cold water, and set aside until required.

2 Put the bread crumbs, milk, and 3 tablespoons of the remaining olive oil in a food processor and process until blended.

3 Add the spinach and ricotta cheese to the food processor and process to a smooth mixture. Transfer the mixture to a bowl, stir in the nutmeg, and season to taste.

4 Mix the tomatoes, garlic, and remaining oil together in a bowl and spoon the mixture into the base of a large ovenproof dish.

5 Fill the lumache with the spinach and ricotta mixture using a teaspoon, then arrange the pasta shells on top of the tomato mixture in the ovenproof dish. Cover and bake in a preheated oven, 350°F/180°C, for 20 minutes. Serve the lumache hot, straight from the oven.

tricolor timballini

serves four

1 tbsp butter, for greasing

1 cup dried white bread crumbs

6 oz/175 g dried tricolor spaghetti,
    broken into 2-inch/5-cm lengths

3 tbsp olive oil

1 egg yolk

1 cup grated Swiss cheese

1¼ cups Béchamel Sauce
    (see page 206)

1 onion, chopped finely

1 bay leaf

⅔ cup dry white wine

⅔ cup bottled strained tomatoes

1 tbsp tomato paste

salt and pepper

fresh basil leaves, to garnish

1 Grease four ¾-cup molds or ramekins with the butter, then evenly coat the insides with half of the bread crumbs.

2 Bring a pan of lightly salted water to a boil. Add the spaghetti and 1 tablespoon of oil, bring back to a boil, and cook for 8–10 minutes, or until just tender but still firm to the bite. Drain and transfer to a mixing bowl. Add the egg yolk and cheese to the pasta and season to taste.

3 Pour the béchamel sauce into the bowl containing the pasta and mix. Spoon the mixture into the ramekins and sprinkle over the remaining bread crumbs.

4 Stand the ramekins on a cookie sheet and bake in a preheated oven, 425°F/220°C, for 20 minutes. Remove from the oven and let stand for 10 minutes.

5 Meanwhile, heat the remaining oil in a pan, add the onion and bay leaf, and cook over low heat for 2–3 minutes.

6 Stir in the wine, tomatoes, and tomato paste, and season with salt and pepper to taste. Simmer gently for 20 minutes, until thickened. Remove and discard the bay leaf.

7 Turn the timballini out onto serving plates, garnish with basil, and serve with the tomato sauce.

pasta baked with three cheeses

VARIATION

Try substituting smoked Bavarian
cheese for the mozzarella or
halloumi and grated colby
cheese for the Parmesan, for a
slightly different, but just as
delicious flavor.

---

1 Lightly grease a large ovenproof dish with the butter.

2 Bring a large pan of lightly salted water to a boil. Add the penne and olive oil, bring back to a boil, and cook for 8–10 minutes, until just tender but still firm to the bite. Drain the pasta, set aside, and keep warm.

3 Beat the eggs into the ricotta cheese and season to taste.

4 Spoon half of the penne into the base of the prepared dish and cover with half of the basil leaves.

5 Spoon half of the ricotta cheese mixture over the pasta. Sprinkle over the grated mozzarella or halloumi cheese and top with the remaining basil leaves. Cover with the remaining penne, then spoon over the remaining ricotta cheese mixture. Lightly sprinkle the freshly grated Parmesan cheese over the top.

6 Bake in a preheated oven, 375°F/190°C, for 30–40 minutes, until golden brown and the cheese topping is bubbling. Garnish with fresh basil leaves, if you like, and serve hot straight from the dish.

baked macaroni

serves four

4 cups dried short-cut macaroni

1 tbsp olive oil

4 tbsp beef drippings

1 lb/450 g potatoes, sliced thinly

1 lb/450 g onions, sliced

2 cups grated mozzarella cheese

⅔ cup heavy cream

salt and pepper

crusty brown bread and butter,
  to serve

VARIATION

For a stronger flavor, use
mozzarella affumicata, a
smoked version of this cheese,
or Swiss cheese, instead of
the normal mozzarella.

1 Bring a large pan of lightly salted water to a boil. Add the macaroni and olive oil, bring back to a boil, and cook for about 12 minutes, or until tender but still firm to the bite. Drain thoroughly and set aside.

2 Melt the beef drippings in a large flameproof casserole over a low heat, then remove the casserole from the heat.

3 Make alternate layers of potatoes, onions, macaroni, and grated mozzarella in the casserole, seasoning well with salt and pepper between each layer and finishing with a layer of cheese on top. Finally, pour the cream over the top layer of cheese.

4 Bake in a preheated oven, 400°F/200°C, for 25 minutes. Remove the casserole from the oven and carefully brown the top under a preheated hot broiler.

5 Serve the macaroni straight from the casserole with crusty brown bread and butter as a filling snack or as a vegetable accompaniment with your favorite entrée.

pancetta & romano cakes

serves four

2 tbsp butter, plus extra
   for greasing

3 ½ oz/100 g pancetta,
   rind removed

scant 2 cups self-rising flour

¾ cup grated romano cheese

⅔ cup milk, plus extra for glazing

1 tsp Worcestershire sauce

1 tbsp tomato catsup

14 oz/400 g dried farfalle pasta

1 tbsp olive oil

salt

TO SERVE

3 tbsp Pesto Sauce (see page 7)
   or anchovy sauce, optional

salad greens, to serve

1 Grease a cookie sheet with a little butter. Cook the pancetta under a preheated broiler until it is cooked. Let cool, then chop finely.

2 Strain the flour and a pinch of salt into a mixing bowl. Add the butter and rub in with your fingertips until the mixture resembles bread crumbs, then add the pancetta and ¼ cup of the grated romano cheese, and stir to blend.

3 In a separate bowl, combine the milk, Worcestershire sauce, and tomato catsup, then add to the dry ingredients. Bring together with your fingers to form a soft dough.

4 Roll out the dough on a lightly floured counter to make a 7-inch/18-cm circle. Brush with a little milk to glaze and cut into 8 wedges.

5 Arrange the dough wedges on the prepared cookie sheet and sprinkle over the remaining cheese. Bake in a preheated oven, 400°F/ 200°C, for 20 minutes.

6 Meanwhile, bring a pan of lightly salted water to a boil. Add the farfalle and the oil, bring back to a boil, and cook for 8–10 minutes, until just tender, but still firm to the bite. Drain and transfer to a large serving dish. Top with the pancetta and romano cakes. Serve with the sauce of your choice and salad greens.

garlic & pine nut tarts

serves four

4 slices of whole-wheat or
    multigrain bread

½ cup pine nuts

¾ cup butter

5 garlic cloves, cut in half

2 tbsp chopped fresh oregano

4 pitted black olives, cut in half

fresh oregano leaves, to garnish

VARIATION

Puff pastry dough can be used
for the tarts. Use 7 oz/200 g
dough to line 4 tartlet pans. Chill
in the refrigerator for 20 minutes.
Line with foil and bake blind for
10 minutes. Remove the foil and
bake for 3–4 minutes, or until
the dough is set. Cool, then
continue from step 2, adding
2 tablespoons fresh bread
crumbs to the mixture instead
of the bread trimmings.

1 Flatten the bread slightly using a
rolling pin, then stamp out
4 circles of bread to fit your individual
tartlet pans, using a cookie cutter
about 4 inches/10 cm wide. Reserve
the bread trimmings and chill them in
the refrigerator for 10 minutes, or
until required.

2 Meanwhile, place the pine nuts
on a cookie sheet and toast them
under a preheated medium broiler for
2–3 minutes, or until golden.

3 Place the bread trimmings, pine
nuts, butter, garlic, and oregano
in a food processor and process for
about 20 seconds. Alternatively, pound
the ingredients by hand in a mortar
with a pestle. The mixture should have
a coarse texture.

4 Spoon the mixture into the bread-
lined pans and top with the olive
halves. Bake in a preheated oven,
400°F/200°C, for 10–15 minutes, or
until golden.

5 Transfer the tarts to serving plates
and serve warm, garnished with
fresh oregano leaves.

provencal tart

serves six

9 oz/250 g ready-made puff pastry
   dough, thawed if frozen

3 tbsp olive oil

2 red bell peppers, seeded and diced

2 green bell peppers, seeded
   and diced

⅔ cup heavy cream

1 egg

2 zucchini, sliced

salt and pepper

1 Roll out the pie dough on a lightly floured counter and use it to line an 8-inch/20-cm loose-based tart pan. Chill the dough in the refrigerator for 20 minutes.

2 Meanwhile, heat 2 tablespoons of the olive oil in a large skillet. Add the diced red and green bell peppers and cook over low heat, stirring frequently, for about 8 minutes, until softened.

3 Whisk the heavy cream and egg together in a bowl and season to taste with salt and pepper. Stir in the cooked bell peppers.

4 Heat the remaining oil in a separate skillet and cook the zucchini slices over medium heat for 4–5 minutes, stirring frequently, until lightly browned.

5 Pour the egg and bell pepper mixture into the tart shell.

6 Arrange the zucchini slices around the edge of the tart.

7 Bake in a preheated oven, 350°F/180°C, for 35–40 minutes, or until just set and golden brown. Serve hot or cold.

fresh tomato tarts

serves six

9 oz/250 g ready-made puff pastry
  dough, thawed if frozen
1 egg, beaten
2 tbsp Pesto Sauce (see page 7)
6 plum tomatoes, sliced
salt and pepper
fresh thyme leaves,
  to garnish (optional)

1 Roll out the pie dough on a lightly floured counter into a rectangle measuring 12 x 10 inches/30 x 25 cm.

2 Cut the rectangle in half and divide each half into 3 pieces to make 6 even-size rectangles. Chill in the refrigerator for 20 minutes.

3 Lightly score the edges of the pie dough rectangles and brush with the beaten egg.

4 Spread the pesto sauce over the rectangles, dividing it equally among them, leaving 1-inch/2.5-cm borders around the edges.

5 Arrange the tomato slices along the center of each rectangle, on top of the pesto sauce.

6 Season with salt and pepper to taste and lightly sprinkle with fresh thyme leaves, if you like.

7 Bake in a preheated oven, 400°F/200°C, for 15–20 minutes, until well risen and golden brown.

8 Transfer the tomato tarts to warmed serving plates straight from the oven, and serve while they are still piping hot.

155

vegetable pasta nests

serves four

6 oz/175 g dried spaghetti

1 eggplant, cut in half lengthwise, then sliced

1 zucchini, diced

1 red bell pepper, seeded and chopped diagonally

6 tbsp olive oil

2 garlic cloves, crushed

butter, for greasing

4 tbsp butter or margarine, melted

1 tbsp dry white bread crumbs

salt and pepper

fresh parsley sprigs, to garnish

COOK'S TIP

The Italian term *al dente* means "to the bite" and describes cooked pasta that is not too soft and still has a "bite" to it. Start timing the pasta from the moment the water comes back to a boil. Begin testing, by biting a small piece of pasta between your front teeth, about 2 minutes before the specified cooking time is up. Drain as soon as it is ready, or it will become soggy.

1 Bring a pan of water to a boil. Add the spaghetti, bring back to a boil, and cook for 8–10 minutes, until tender but still firm to the bite. Drain and set aside.

2 Place the eggplant, zucchini, and bell pepper on a cookie sheet.

3 Combine the oil and garlic and pour over the vegetables, tossing them to coat well.

4 Cook the vegetables under a preheated hot broiler for about 10 minutes, turning occasionally, until tender and lightly charred. Set aside and keep warm.

5 Lightly grease 4 large, shallow muffin pans and divide the spaghetti between them. Curl the spaghetti to form nests using 2 forks.

6 Brush the pasta nests with melted butter or margarine and sprinkle with the bread crumbs. Bake in a preheated oven, 400°F/200°C, for 15 minutes, or until lightly golden. Remove the pasta nests from the pans and transfer to warmed individual serving plates. Divide the broiled vegetables among the pasta nests, season to taste with salt and pepper, and garnish with sprigs of parsley.

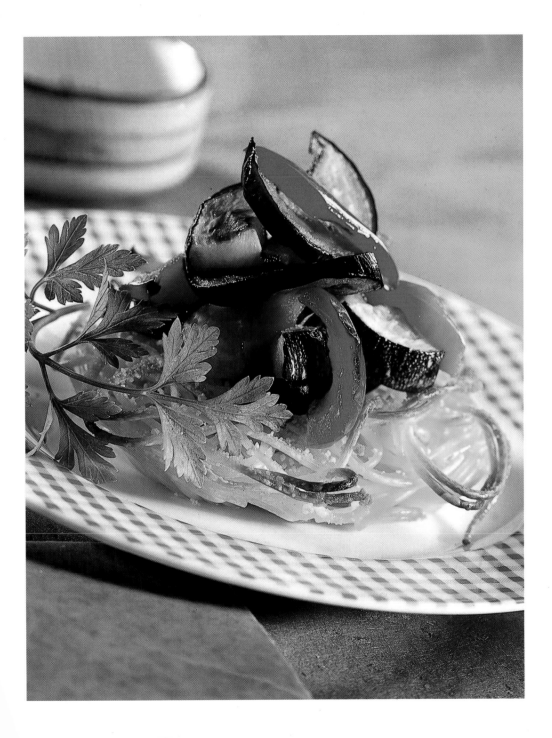

mini cheese & onion tarts

makes twelve

DOUGH

¾ cup all-purpose flour, plus extra
   for dusting

¼ tsp salt

5½ tbsp butter, diced

1–2 tbsp water

FILLING

1 egg, beaten

generous ⅓ cup light cream

½ cup grated Dry Jack or
   colby cheese

3 scallions, chopped finely

salt

cayenne pepper

1 To make the dough, strain the flour and salt into a mixing bowl. Add the butter and rub it in with your fingertips until the mixture resembles bread crumbs. Stir in the water, bring together to form a dough, and shape into a ball. Cover with plastic wrap and chill in the refrigerator for 30 minutes.

2 Roll out the dough on a lightly floured counter. Stamp out 12 circles from the dough using a 3-inch/7.5-cm cookie cutter and use them to line a shallow muffin pan.

3 To make the filling, whisk the beaten egg, cream, grated cheese, and scallions together in a pitcher. Season to taste with salt and cayenne pepper.

4 Pour the filling mixture into the tart shells and bake in a preheated oven, 350°F/180°C, for about 20–25 minutes, or until the filling is just set. Serve hot, or transfer to a wire rack to cool.

ham & cheese lattice pies

serves six

1 tbsp butter, for greasing

9 oz/250 g ready-made puff pastry
    dough, thawed if frozen

generous ⅓ cup finely chopped ham

½ cup soft cheese

2 tbsp chopped fresh chives

1 egg, beaten

scant ½ cup freshly grated
    Parmesan cheese

pepper

1 Lightly grease 2 large cookie sheets with the butter. Roll out the pastry dough on a lightly floured counter, then cut out 12 rectangles of dough measuring 6 x 2 inches/ 15 x 5 cm.

2 Place the rectangles on the prepared cookie sheets and chill in the refrigerator for 30 minutes.

3 Meanwhile, combine the ham, cheese, and chives in a small bowl. Season with pepper to taste.

4 Divide the ham and cheese mixture along the center of 6 of the rectangles, leaving a 1-inch/2.5-cm border around the edges. Brush the borders with the beaten egg.

5 To make the lattice pattern, fold the remaining rectangles lengthwise. Leaving a 1-inch/2.5-cm border, cut vertical lines across the folded edge of the rectangles.

6 Unfold the latticed rectangles and place them over the rectangles topped with the ham and cheese mixture. Press the dough edges to seal them and lightly sprinkle with the grated Parmesan cheese.

7 Bake in a preheated oven, 350°F/ 180°C, for 15–20 minutes. Serve immediately or transfer to a wire rack to cool and serve cold.

159

pissaladière

VARIATION

Cut the pissaladière into squares
or triangles for easy finger food
at a party or barbecue grill.

1 Lightly grease an edged cookie sheet. Heat the olive oil in a large pan. Cook the onions and garlic over low heat for about 30 minutes, stirring occasionally.

2 Add the sugar and red wine vinegar to the pan and season with plenty of salt and pepper.

3 Roll out the dough on a lightly floured counter into a rectangle measuring 13 x 9 inches/33 x 23 cm. Carefully transfer the dough rectangle to the prepared cookie sheet, pushing the dough well into the corners.

4 Spread the onion mixture evenly over the dough.

5 To make the decorative topping, arrange the anchovy fillets in a criss-cross pattern over the top of the onion mixture, then dot with the green olives, and sprinkle the dried marjoram over the top.

6 Bake in a preheated oven, 425°F/ 220°C, for 20–25 minutes, until lightly golden. Serve the pissaladière piping hot, straight from the oven.

tuna-stuffed tomatoes

serves four

4 plum tomatoes

2 tbsp sun-dried tomato paste

2 egg yolks

2 tsp lemon juice

finely grated rind of 1 lemon

4 tbsp olive oil

4 oz/115 g canned tuna, drained

2 tbsp capers, rinsed

salt and pepper

TO GARNISH

2 sun-dried tomatoes in oil, drained
   and cut into strips

fresh basil leaves

1 Halve the tomatoes and scoop out the seeds. Divide the sun-dried tomato paste among the tomato halves and spread around the inside of the skins.

2 Place on a cookie sheet and roast in a preheated oven, 400°F/200°C, for 12–15 minutes. Let cool slightly.

3 To make the mayonnaise, place the egg yolks and lemon juice in a food processor with the lemon rind and process until a smooth mixture forms. With the motor running, gradually add the olive oil. Stop the processor as soon as the mayonnaise has thickened. Alternatively, use a hand whisk to beat the mixture constantly until it thickens.

4 Add the tuna and capers to the mayonnaise, season, and stir.

5 Spoon the tuna mixture into the tomato shells and garnish with sun-dried tomato strips and basil. Return to the oven for a few minutes to warm through, or serve chilled.

baked tuna & ricotta rigatoni

serves four

1 tbsp butter, for greasing

1 lb/450 g dried rigatoni pasta

1 tbsp olive oil

7 oz/200 g canned flaked
  tuna, drained

1 cup ricotta cheese

½ cup heavy cream

2 cups freshly grated
  Parmesan cheese

4½ oz/125 g sun-dried tomatoes in
  oil, drained and sliced

salt and pepper

VARIATION

For a vegetarian alternative to
this recipe, simply substitute a
mixture of pitted and chopped
black olives and chopped
walnuts for the tuna.

1 Lightly grease a large ovenproof
dish with the butter.

2 Bring a large pan of lightly
salted water to a boil. Add the
rigatoni and olive oil, bring back to a
boil, and cook for 8–10 minutes, until
just tender but still firm to the bite.
Drain the pasta and set aside until cool
enough to handle.

3 Meanwhile, combine the flaked
tuna and ricotta cheese in a bowl
until thoroughly blended into a soft
paste. Spoon the mixture into a pastry
bag and use it to fill the rigatoni.
Arrange the filled pasta tubes side by
side in a single layer in the prepared
ovenproof dish.

4 Combine the cream and Parmesan
cheese and season with salt and
pepper to taste.

5 Spoon the cream mixture over
the rigatoni and top with the
sun-dried tomatoes, arranged in a
criss-cross pattern. Bake in a preheated
oven, 400°F/200°C, for 20 minutes.
Serve hot straight from the dish.

roasted seafood & vegetables

serves four

1 lb 5 oz/600 g new potatoes

3 red onions, cut into wedges

2 zucchini, cut into chunks

8 garlic cloves

2 lemons, cut into wedges

4 fresh rosemary sprigs

4 tbsp olive oil

12 oz/350 g shell-on shrimp,
  preferably raw

2 small prepared squid, chopped
  into rings

4 tomatoes, quartered

VARIATION

Most vegetables are suitable for roasting in the oven. Try adding 1 lb/450 g pumpkin, squash, or eggplant, if you like.

1 Scrub the potatoes to remove any dirt. Cut any large potatoes in half. Place the potatoes in a large roasting pan, together with the onions, zucchini, garlic, lemon wedges, and rosemary sprigs.

2 Pour the oil into the roasting pan and toss well to coat the vegetables. Cook in a preheated oven, 400°F/200°C, for about 40 minutes, turning occasionally, until the potatoes are cooked and tender.

3 Once the potatoes are tender, add the shrimp, squid, and tomatoes, tossing to coat them in the oil, and roast for 10 minutes more. All of the vegetables should be cooked through and slightly charred for full flavor, and the shrimp should have turned pink.

4 Transfer the roasted seafood and vegetables to warmed serving plates using a slotted spoon, and serve immediately.

Savory Entrées

This chapter presents a mouthwatering array of savory dishes to tempt any palate, including pies, pastries, tarts, and flans, as well as a variety of delicious savory bakes. The choice is wide, including Baked Cheese Cream, Red Onion Tart Tatin, and Asparagus & Cheese Tart. Fish fans can choose from a wide menu, including Smoky Fish Pie, Fresh Baked Sardines, and Fillets of Red Snapper & Pasta. Meat and poultry dishes include Red Roast Pork in Soy Sauce, Fruity Lamb Casserole, and Italian Chicken Parcels.

vermicelli & vegetable tart

serves four

6 tbsp butter, plus extra for greasing

8 oz/225 g dried vermicelli
    or spaghetti

1 tbsp olive oil

1 onion, chopped

5 oz/140 g white mushrooms

1 green bell pepper, seeded, and
    sliced into thin rings

⅔ cup milk

3 eggs, beaten lightly

2 tbsp heavy cream

1 tsp dried oregano

freshly grated nutmeg

¼ cup freshly grated
    Parmesan cheese

salt and pepper

tomato and basil salad,
    to serve (optional)

1 Generously grease an 8-inch/ 20-cm loose-based tart pan with a little butter.

2 Bring a large pan of lightly salted water to a boil. Add the vermicelli or spaghetti and olive oil, bring back to a boil, and cook for 8–10 minutes, until tender but still firm to the bite. Drain, return to the pan, add 2 tablespoons of the butter, and shake the pan to coat the pasta.

3 Press the pasta onto the base and around the sides of the tart pan to make a tart shell, pressing the center down to make a hollow.

4 Melt the remaining butter in a large skillet over medium heat. Add the chopped onion and cook until it is translucent.

5 Add the mushrooms and bell pepper rings to the skillet. Cook, stirring constantly, for 2–3 minutes. Spoon the onion, mushroom, and bell pepper mixture into the pasta tart shell and press it evenly into the base.

6 Beat together the milk, eggs, and cream, stir in the oregano, and season to taste with nutmeg and pepper. Carefully pour the mixture over the vegetables, then sprinkle with the Parmesan cheese.

7 Bake in a preheated oven, 350°F/180°C, for 40–45 minutes, or until the filling has set.

8 Carefully slide the tart out of the pan onto a serving platter and serve warm with a tomato and basil salad, if you like.

asparagus & cheese tart

serves six

9 oz/250 g ready-made pie dough,
    thawed if frozen
9 oz/250 g asparagus
1 tbsp vegetable oil
1 red onion, chopped finely
2 tbsp chopped hazelnuts
7 oz/200 g goat cheese
2 eggs, beaten
4 tbsp light cream
salt and pepper

1 Roll out the pie dough on a lightly floured counter and use it to line a 9½-inch/24-cm loose-based tart pan. Prick the base of the tart shell with a fork and chill in the refrigerator for 30 minutes.

2 Line the tart shell with foil and baking beans and bake in a preheated oven, 375°F/190°C, for about 15 minutes.

3 Remove the foil and baking beans and bake for 15 minutes more.

4 Cook the asparagus in boiling water for 2–3 minutes, drain, and cut into bite-size pieces.

5 Heat the oil in a small skillet. Add the onion and cook over low heat, stirring occasionally, until soft and lightly golden. Spoon the asparagus, onion, and hazelnuts into the prepared tart shell.

6 Beat the cheese, eggs, and cream together in a bowl until smooth, or place in a food processor and process until smooth. Season well with salt and pepper, then pour over the mixture in the tart shell.

7 Bake in the preheated oven for 15–20 minutes, or until the filling is just set. Serve warm or cold.

VARIATION
Omit the hazelnuts and sprinkle Parmesan cheese over the top of the tart just before cooking, if you like.

baked cheese cream

serves four

1 tbsp butter, for greasing

2½ cups fresh white bread crumbs

1 cup grated Swiss cheese

⅔ cup lukewarm milk

½ cup butter, melted

2 eggs, separated

2 tbsp chopped fresh parsley

salt and pepper

salad greens, to serve

1 Grease a 4-cup/1-litre ovenproof dish with the butter.

2 Combine the bread crumbs and cheese in a bowl. Pour the milk over the cheese and bread crumb mixture and stir to blend. Add the melted butter, egg yolks, parsley, and salt and pepper to taste and mix.

3 In a separate bowl, whisk the egg whites until they form soft peaks. Gently fold the cheese mixture into the egg whites, using a figure-eight movement.

4 Transfer the mixture to the prepared ovenproof dish and smooth the surface with a spatula.

5 Bake in a preheated oven, 375°F/ 190°C, for 45 minutes, or until golden and slightly risen, and a fine metal skewer inserted into the middle of the dish comes out clean.

6 Serve the baked cheese cream piping hot, straight from the dish, with salad greens.

red onion tart tatin

serves four

4 tbsp butter

2 tbsp sugar

1 lb 2 oz/500 g red onions, cut
   into fourths

3 tbsp red wine vinegar

2 tbsp fresh thyme leaves

9 oz/250 g ready-made puff pastry
   dough, thawed if frozen

salt and pepper

VARIATION

Replace the red onions with
shallots, leaving them whole,
if you like.

COOK'S TIP

A heavy, cast iron skillet is best
for making this classic upside-
down tart, as it distributes the
heat evenly so that the onions
will not stick.

---

1 Place the butter and sugar in a 9-inch/23-cm ovenproof skillet and cook over medium heat until the butter has melted and the sugar has dissolved.

2 Add the red onion fourths and sweat over low heat for about 10–15 minutes, stirring occasionally, until golden and caramelized.

3 Add the red wine vinegar and thyme leaves to the skillet. Season to taste, then simmer over medium heat until the liquid has reduced and the red onion pieces are coated in the buttery sauce.

4 Roll out the dough on a lightly floured counter into a circle slightly larger than the skillet.

5 Place the dough over the onion mixture in the skillet and press down, tucking in the edges to seal.

6 Bake in a preheated oven, 350°F/180°C, for 20–25 minutes, until the dough is firm and golden Remove the skillet from the oven and let the tart stand for 10 minutes.

7 To turn out, place a serving plate over the skillet and, holding them firmly together, carefully invert so that the pastry becomes the base of the tart. Serve the tart warm.

celery & onion pies

makes twelve

DOUGH

1 cup all-purpose flour, plus extra
    for dusting

½ tsp salt

2 tbsp butter, diced

¼ cup grated sharp cheese

3–4 tbsp water

FILLING

2 tbsp butter

1 cup finely chopped celery

2 garlic cloves, crushed

1 small onion, chopped finely

1 tbsp all-purpose flour

¼ cup milk

salt

pinch of cayenne pepper

1 To make the filling, melt the butter in a large skillet. Add the celery, garlic, and onion and cook over low heat, stirring occasionally, for about 5 minutes, or until softened.

2 Reduce the heat and stir in the flour, then the milk. Bring back to a simmer, then cook gently over low heat until the mixture is thick, stirring frequently. Season with salt and cayenne pepper to taste and let cool.

3 To make the dough, strain the flour and salt into a bowl and rub in the butter with your fingertips. Stir in the cheese and the cold water, and bring together to form a dough.

4 Roll out three-fourths of the dough on a lightly floured counter. Stamp out 12 circles using a 2½-inch/6-cm cookie cutter. Line a patty pan with the dough circles.

5 Divide the filling between the dough circles. Roll out the remaining dough and, using a 2-inch/5-cm cutter, stamp out 12 circles. Place the smaller circles on top of the pie filling and press to seal. Make a slit in each pie and chill in the refrigerator for 30 minutes.

6 Bake in a preheated oven, 425°F/220°C, for 15–20 minutes. Let cool in the pan for 10 minutes before turning out. Serve warm.

onion tart

serves four

9 oz/250 g ready-made pie dough,
    thawed if frozen

3 tbsp butter

generous ⅓ cup chopped bacon

1 lb 9 oz/700 g onions,
    thinly sliced

2 eggs, beaten

scant ⅔ cup freshly grated
    Parmesan cheese

1 tsp dried sage

salt and pepper

VARIATION

To make a vegetarian version
of this tart, replace the bacon
with the same amount of
chopped mushrooms.

1 Roll out the pie dough on a lightly floured counter and use it to line a 9½-inch/24-cm loose-based tart pan.

2 Prick the base of the tart shell with a fork and chill in the refrigerator for 30 minutes.

3 Meanwhile, heat the butter in a pan, add the bacon and onions, and sweat over low heat for about 25 minutes, or until tender. If the onion slices start to brown, add 1 tablespoon of water to the pan.

4 Add the beaten eggs to the onion mixture and stir in the grated cheese and sage. Season with salt and pepper to taste.

5 Spoon the onion mixture into the prepared tart shell, spreading it out evenly over the base.

6 Bake in a preheated oven, 350°F/ 180°C, for 20–30 minutes, or until the filling has just set and the pastry is crisp and golden.

7 Let the tart cool slightly in the pan. Serve warm or cold.

gorgonzola & pumpkin pizza

serves four

PIZZA DOUGH

¼ oz/10 g active dry yeast

1 tsp sugar

1 cup lukewarm water

1¼ cups whole-wheat all-purpose flour, plus extra for dusting

1¼ cups white bread flour

1 tsp salt

1 tbsp olive oil, plus extra for brushing

1 fresh rosemary sprig, to garnish

TOPPING

14 oz/400 g pumpkin or squash, peeled and cubed

1 tbsp olive oil

1 pear, cored, peeled, and sliced

3½ oz/100 g Gorgonzola cheese

1 Place the yeast and sugar in a medium pitcher and mix with 4 tablespoons of the lukewarm water. Let the yeast mixture stand in a warm place for 15 minutes, or until frothy.

2 Combine both of the flours with the salt and make a well in the center. Add the oil, yeast mixture, and remaining water. Bring together using a wooden spoon to form a dough.

3 Turn the dough out onto a floured counter and knead for 4–5 minutes, or until smooth.

4 Return the dough to the bowl and cover with an oiled sheet of plastic wrap. Let rise for 30 minutes or until doubled in size.

5 Brush a cookie sheet with oil. Punch down the dough for 2 minutes. Roll out the dough into a long oval shape, then place it on the cookie sheet, and push out the edges until even. The dough should be no more than ¼ inch/5 mm thick because it will rise during cooking.

6 To make the topping, place the pumpkin in a shallow roasting pan. Drizzle with the olive oil and cook under a preheated medium broiler for 20 minutes, or until lightly golden.

7 Arrange the pear and pumpkin on top of the dough, brushing with the oil from the roasting pan. Crumble over the Gorgonzola. Bake in a preheated oven, 400°F/200°C, for 15 minutes, or until the base is golden. Garnish with a sprig of rosemary.

stuffed eggplant

serves four

8 oz/225 g dried penne pasta

4 tbsp olive oil, plus extra
   for brushing

2 eggplant

1 large onion, chopped

2 garlic cloves, crushed

14 oz/400 g canned
   chopped tomatoes

2 tsp dried oregano

2 oz/55 g mozzarella cheese,
   sliced thinly

⅓ cup freshly grated
   Parmesan cheese

2 tbsp dry white or whole-wheat
   bread crumbs

salt and pepper

salad greens, to serve

1 Bring a pan of lightly salted water to a boil. Add the pasta and 1 tablespoon of the olive oil, bring back to a boil, and cook for 8–10 minutes, or until tender but still firm to the bite. Drain, return to the pan, cover, and keep warm.

2 Cut the eggplant in half lengthwise and score around the inside with a sharp knife, being careful not to pierce the shells. Scoop out the pulp with a spoon. Brush the insides of the shells with olive oil. Chop the pulp and set aside.

3 Heat the remaining oil in a skillet. Cook the onion until translucent. Add the garlic and cook for 1 minute. Add the chopped eggplant pulp and cook, stirring frequently, for 5 minutes. Add the tomatoes and oregano and season to taste. Bring to a boil and simmer for 10 minutes, or until thickened. Remove the skillet from the heat and stir in the pasta.

4 Brush a cookie sheet with oil and arrange the eggplant shells on the sheet in a single layer. Divide half of the tomato and pasta mixture

among them. Sprinkle over the mozzarella, then pile the remaining tomato and pasta mixture on top. Mix the Parmesan cheese and bread crumbs in a small bowl and sprinkle over the top, patting lightly into the stuffing mixture.

5 Bake the stuffed eggplant in a preheated oven, 400°F/200°C, for 25 minutes, or until the topping is golden brown. Serve hot with a selection of salad greens.

smoky fish pie

serves four

2 lb/900 g smoked haddock or
cod fillets

2½ cups skim milk

2 bay leaves

4 oz/115 g white mushrooms, cut
into fourths

1 cup frozen peas

⅔ cup frozen corn kernels

4 cups diced potatoes

5 tbsp lowfat plain yogurt

4 tbsp chopped fresh parsley

2 oz/60 g smoked salmon, sliced
into thin strips

3 tbsp cornstarch

¼ cup grated smoked cheese

salt and pepper

1 Place the fish in a large pan and
add the milk and bay leaves.
Bring to a boil, cover, then reduce the
heat, and simmer for 5 minutes. Add
the mushrooms, peas, and corn, bring
back to a simmer, cover, and cook for
5–7 minutes. Let cool.

2 Place the potatoes in a pan, cover
with water, bring to a boil, and
cook for 8 minutes. Drain well and
mash with a fork or potato masher. Stir
in the yogurt, parsley and seasoning
and set aside.

3 Using a slotted spoon, remove
the fish from the pan. Flake the
cooked fish away from the skin and
place in a gratin dish.

4 Drain the mushrooms, peas,
and corn, reserving the cooking
liquid. Gently stir into the fish with the
salmon strips.

5 Blend a little cooking liquid into
the cornstarch to make a paste.
Transfer the rest of the cooking liquid
to a pan and add the paste. Heat
through, stirring, until thickened.
Discard the bay leaves and season to
taste with salt and pepper. Pour the
sauce over the fish and vegetables
and stir to mix. Spoon the mashed
potato on top and spread to cover
the fish, sprinkle with cheese, and bake
in a preheated oven, 400°F/200°C, for
25–30 minutes.

pasta & shrimp parcels

serves four

1 lb/450 g dried fettuccine pasta

⅔ cup Pesto Sauce (see page 7)

4 tsp extra virgin olive oil

1 lb 10 oz/750 g jumbo shrimp,
    peeled and deveined

2 garlic cloves, crushed

½ cup dry white wine

salt and pepper

wedges of lemon, to garnish

COOK'S TIP

Traditionally, these parcels are
designed to look like money
bags. The resemblance is more
effective with waxed paper
rather than with foil.

1 Cut 4 squares, 12 inches/30 cm
wide, out of waxed paper.

2 Bring a large pan of lightly
salted water to a boil. Add the
fettuccine and cook for 2–3 minutes,
until just softened. Drain thoroughly.

3 Mix the fettuccine with half of the
pesto sauce. Spread out the paper
squares and place 1 teaspoon of olive
oil in the center of each. Divide the
fettuccine among the squares, then
divide the shrimp, and place on top
of the fettuccine.

4 Mix the remaining pesto sauce
with the garlic in a small bowl
and spoon it over the shrimp. Season
each parcel with salt and pepper and
sprinkle with the white wine.

5 Dampen the edges of the waxed
paper and bring them together to
wrap the parcels loosely, twisting the
edges to seal.

6 Place the parcels on a cookie sheet
and bake in a preheated oven,
400°F/200°C, for 10–15 minutes,
until piping hot and the shrimp have
changed color. Transfer the parcels to
serving plates, garnish with lemon
wedges, and serve.

baked macaroni & shrimp

serves four

12 oz/350 g short pasta, such as
   short-cut macaroni
1 tbsp olive oil, plus extra
   for brushing
6 tbsp butter, plus extra for greasing
2 small fennel bulbs, thinly sliced,
   leaves reserved
2½ cups thinly sliced mushrooms
6 oz/175 g shelled, cooked shrimp
2½ cups Béchamel Sauce
   (see page 206)
pinch of cayenne pepper
⅔ cup freshly grated
   Parmesan cheese
2 large tomatoes, sliced
1 tsp dried oregano
salt

1 Bring a large pan of lightly salted water to a boil. Add the pasta and olive oil, bring back to a boil, and cook for 8–10 minutes, or until tender but still firm to the bite. Drain the pasta, return to the pan, and dot with 2 tablespoons of the butter. Shake the pan well to coat the pasta, cover, and keep warm.

2 Melt the remaining butter in a large skillet over medium heat, add the fennel, and cook for about 3–4 minutes, until it begins to soften. Stir in the mushrooms and cook, stirring, for 2 minutes. Stir in the cooked shrimp, remove the pan from the heat, and set aside until required.

3 Season the hot béchamel sauce to taste with a pinch of cayenne. Stir the reserved fennel, mushroom, and shrimp mixture into the sauce, then stir in the pasta.

4 Grease a round, shallow ovenproof dish with a little butter. Pour in the pasta mixture and spread evenly over the base of the dish. Sprinkle with the Parmesan cheese and arrange the tomato slices in a ring around the edge of the dish. Brush the tomato with olive oil and sprinkle with the dried oregano.

5 Bake in a preheated oven, 350°F/180°C, for 25 minutes, or until golden. Serve hot.

seafood lasagna

serves four

1 lb/450 g smoked haddock fillets
skin removed and flesh flaked

4 oz/115 g shrimp

4 oz/115 g sole fillet, skin removed
and flesh sliced

juice of 1 lemon

4 tbsp butter

3 leeks, sliced very thinly

scant ½ cup all-purpose flour

2⅓ cups milk

2 tbsp honey

2 cups grated mozzarella cheese

1 lb/450 g pre-cooked lasagna

⅔ cup freshly grated
Parmesan cheese

pepper

1 Put the haddock, shrimp, and
sole into a large mixing bowl and
season with pepper and lemon juice
according to taste. Set aside while you
make the sauce.

2 Melt the butter in a large pan
over low heat. Add the leeks and
cook, stirring occasionally, for about
8 minutes, until softened. Add the
flour and cook, stirring constantly, for
1 minute. Gradually stir in enough milk
to make a thick, creamy sauce.

3 Thoroughly blend in the honey
and mozzarella cheese and cook
the sauce for 3 minutes more, then
remove the pan from the heat, and mix
in the seasoned haddock, sole, and
shrimp mixture.

4 Place a layer of fish sauce in an
ovenproof dish, followed by a
layer of lasagna, and continue with
alternate layers, finishing with a layer
of fish sauce on top. Generously
sprinkle over the grated Parmesan
cheese and bake the lasagna in a
preheated oven, 350°F/180°C, for
30 minutes. Serve immediately.

VARIATION

For a hard cider sauce,
substitute 1 finely chopped
shallot for the leeks, 1½ cups of
hard cider and 1½ cups of
heavy cream for the milk, and
1 teaspoon of mustard for the
honey. For a Tuscan sauce,
substitute 1 chopped fennel bulb
for the leeks and omit the honey.

smoked haddock casserole

serves four

2 tbsp butter, plus extra for greasing

1 lb/450 g smoked haddock fillets,
    cut into 4 portions

2½ cups milk

scant ¼ cup all-purpose flour

pinch of freshly grated nutmeg

3 tbsp heavy cream

1 tbsp chopped fresh parsley

2 eggs, hard-cooked and mashed
    to a pulp

1 lb/450 g dried fusilli pasta

1 tbsp lemon juice

salt and pepper

fresh flatleaf parsley, to garnish

TO SERVE

boiled new potatoes

beets

VARIATION

Try using penne, conchiglie, or
rigatoni for this casserole.

---

1 Generously grease a casserole with butter. Put the haddock in the casserole and pour over the milk. Bake in a preheated oven, 400°F/200°C, for about 15 minutes, until tender and the flesh flakes easily.

2 Carefully pour off the cooking liquid into a pitcher without breaking up the fish and reserve. The fish should remain in the casserole.

3 Melt the butter in a pan and stir in the flour. Gradually whisk in the cooking liquid. Season with salt, pepper, and nutmeg. Stir in the cream, chopped parsley, and mashed eggs and cook, stirring, for 2 minutes.

4 Meanwhile, bring a large pan of lightly salted water to a boil. Add the fusilli and lemon juice, bring back to a boil, and cook for 8–10 minutes, until tender but still firm to the bite.

5 Drain the pasta and spoon or tip it over the fish. Top with the egg sauce and return the casserole to the oven for 10 minutes.

6 Transfer the haddock casserole to serving plates, garnish with flatleaf parsley, and serve piping hot with boiled new potatoes and beets.

fresh baked sardines

serves four

2 tbsp olive oil

2 large onions, sliced into rings

3 garlic cloves, chopped

2 large zucchini, cut into sticks

3 tbsp fresh thyme leaves

8 sardine fillets or about
    2 lb 4 oz/1 kg sardines, filleted

1 cup freshly grated
    Parmesan cheese

4 eggs, beaten

1¼ cups milk

salt and pepper.

VARIATION

If you cannot find sardines that are large enough to fillet, use small mackerel instead.

1 Heat 1 tablespoon of the olive oil in a skillet. Add the onions and garlic and cook over low heat, stirring occasionally, for 2–3 minutes, until soft and translucent.

2 Add the zucchini to the skillet and cook, stirring occasionally, for about 5 minutes, or until turning golden. Stir 2 tablespoons of the thyme leaves into the mixture and remove from the heat.

3 Place half of the onion and zucchini mixture in the base of a large ovenproof dish. Top with the sardine fillets and half of the Parmesan cheese. Place the remaining onions and zucchini on top and sprinkle with the remaining thyme.

4 Combine the eggs and milk in a bowl and season to taste with salt and pepper. Pour the mixture into the dish and sprinkle the remaining Parmesan cheese over the top.

5 Bake in a preheated oven, 350°F/ 180°C, for about 20–25 minutes, or until golden and set. Serve the sardines hot.

trout with smoked bacon

serves four

1 tbsp butter, for greasing

4 whole trout, about 9½ oz/275 g
    each, gutted and cleaned

12 anchovies in oil, drained
    and chopped

2 apples, peeled, cored, and sliced

4 fresh mint sprigs

juice of 1 lemon

12 strips of smoked lean bacon

1 lb/450 g dried tagliatelle

1 tbsp olive oil

salt and pepper

TO GARNISH

2 apples, cored and sliced

4 fresh mint sprigs

1 Grease a deep cookie sheet with
the butter.

2 Open up the cavities of each trout
and rinse with warm salt water.

3 Season each cavity with salt and
pepper. Divide the anchovies,
sliced apples, and mint sprigs among
the cavities. Sprinkle the lemon juice
into each cavity.

4 Carefully wrap 3 strips of smoked
bacon around the whole of each
trout, except the head and tail, in a
spiral. Tuck the loose ends of bacon
underneath to secure them.

5 Arrange the trout on the prepared
cookie sheet. Season with pepper.
Bake in a preheated oven, 400°F/
200°C, for 20 minutes, turning the
trout over after 10 minutes.

6 Meanwhile, bring a large pan
of lightly salted water to a boil.
Add the tagliatelle and olive oil, bring
back to a boil, and cook for about
12 minutes, until tender but still firm
to the bite. Drain and transfer to a
warmed serving dish.

7 Remove the trout from the oven
and arrange on the tagliatelle.
Garnish with sliced apples and fresh
mint sprigs and serve immediately.

spaghetti alla bucaniera

serves four

¾ cup all-purpose flour

1 lb/450 g flounder or sole fillets, skinned and chopped

1 lb/450 g hake fillets, skinned and chopped

6 tbsp butter

4 shallots, chopped finely

2 garlic cloves, crushed

1 carrot, diced

1 leek, chopped finely

1¼ cups hard cider

1¼ cups medium sweet cider

2 tsp anchovy paste

1 tbsp tarragon vinegar

1 lb/450 g dried spaghetti

1 tbsp olive oil

salt and pepper

chopped fresh parsley, to garnish

crusty brown bread, to serve

1 Season the flour with salt and pepper. Sprinkle ¼ cup of the seasoned flour onto a shallow plate. Press the fish pieces into the seasoned flour to coat thoroughly all over. Alternatively, put the flour in a plastic bag, add the fish pieces, a few at a time, and shake gently.

2 Melt the butter in a flameproof casserole. Add the fish fillets, shallots, garlic, carrot, and leek and cook over low heat, stirring frequently, for about 10 minutes.

3 Sprinkle over the remaining seasoned flour and cook, stirring constantly, for 2 minutes. Gradually stir in the cider, anchovy paste, and tarragon vinegar and bring to a boil. Cover the casserole, transfer to a preheated oven, 350°F/180°C, and bake for 30 minutes.

4 About 15 minutes before the end of the cooking time, bring a large pan of lightly salted water to a boil. Add the spaghetti and olive oil, bring back to a boil, and cook for about 12 minutes, until tender but still firm to the bite. Drain the pasta and transfer to a large, warmed serving dish.

5 Arrange the baked fish mixture on top of the spaghetti in the serving dish and pour over any remaining sauce. Garnish with chopped parsley and serve immediately with warm, crusty brown bread.

cannelloni filetti di sogliola

serves six

12 small fillets of sole, about
    4 oz/115 g each

⅔ cup red wine

6 tbsp butter

1⅔ cups sliced white mushrooms

4 shallots, chopped finely

4 oz/115 g tomatoes, chopped

2 tbsp tomato paste

scant ½ cup all-purpose
    flour, strained

⅔ cup warm milk

2 tbsp heavy cream

6 dried cannelloni tubes

6 oz/175 g cooked, peeled
    freshwater shrimp

salt and pepper

1 fresh fennel frond, to garnish

1 Brush the sole fillets with a little wine, season with salt and pepper, and roll up, skin side inward. Secure with a toothpick or skewer.

2 Arrange the fish rolls in a single layer in a large skillet, add the remaining red wine, and poach for 4 minutes. Remove the fish from the pan and reserve the liquid.

3 Melt the butter in a separate pan, add the mushrooms and shallots, and cook for 2 minutes, then add the tomatoes and tomato paste. Season the flour and stir it into the pan. Stir in the reserved cooking liquid and half of the milk. Cook over low heat, stirring, for 4 minutes. Remove from the heat and stir in the cream.

4 Bring a large pan of lightly salted water to a boil. Add the cannelloni, bring back to a boil, and cook for 8 minutes, until tender but still firm to the bite. Drain and let cool.

5 Remove the toothpicks or skewers from the fish rolls. Put 2 fish rolls into each cannelloni tube with 2 or 3 shrimp and a little red wine sauce. Arrange the cannelloni in a single layer in an ovenproof dish, pour over the red wine sauce, and bake in a preheated oven, 400°F/200°C, for 20 minutes, until cooked through and piping hot.

6 Serve the cannelloni with the red wine sauce, garnished with the remaining shrimp and a fennel frond.

190

orange mackerel

serves four

2 tbsp vegetable oil

4 scallions, chopped

2 oranges

scant ½ cup ground almonds

1 tbsp oats

½ cup mixed pitted green and black
olives, chopped

8 mackerel fillets

salt and pepper

salad greens, to serve

1 Heat the oil in a skillet. Add the scallions and cook over low heat for 2 minutes, stirring frequently, then set aside.

2 Finely grate the rind of the oranges, then, using a sharp knife, cut away the remaining skin and the white pith.

3 Using a sharp knife, segment the oranges by cutting down either side of the membranes to loosen each segment. Do this over a plate so that you can catch and reserve any juices. Cut each orange segment in half.

4 Lightly toast the almonds under a preheated medium broiler for 2–3 minutes, or until golden; watch them carefully as they brown quickly.

5 Combine the scallions, orange rind and segments, ground almonds, oats, and olives in a bowl and season with salt and pepper.

6 Lay the mackerel fillets in an ovenproof dish. Spoon the orange mixture along the center of each, then roll up and secure with toothpicks.

7 Bake in a preheated oven, 375°F/190°C for 25 minutes, until the fish is tender and cooked through.

8 Transfer the mackerel to warmed serving plates and remove and discard the toothpicks. Serve warm with salad greens.

italian cod

serves four

2 tbsp butter

1 cup fresh whole-wheat
bread crumbs

2 tbsp chopped walnuts

grated rind and juice of 2 lemons

2 fresh rosemary sprigs,
stems removed

2 tbsp chopped fresh parsley

4 cod fillets, about 5½ oz/150 g each

1 garlic clove, crushed

1 small fresh red chile, seeded
and diced

3 tbsp walnut oil

salad greens, to serve

VARIATION

If you like, the walnuts may
be omitted from the crust. In
addition, extra virgin olive oil
can be used instead of walnut
oil, if you like.

1 Melt the butter in a large pan
over low heat.

2 Remove the pan from the heat
and stir in the bread crumbs and
walnuts, the rind and juice of 1 lemon,
half of the fresh rosemary, and half of
the fresh parsley.

3 Line a roasting pan with foil and
place the cod fillets in the pan in
a single layer. Gently press the bread
crumb mixture over the top of the cod
fillets with your fingers.

4 Bake in a preheated oven,
400°F/200°C, for 25–30 minutes.

5 Place the garlic, the remaining
lemon rind and juice, rosemary
and parsley in a bowl with the chile
and mix. Beat in the walnut oil. Drizzle
the dressing over the cod steaks as
soon as they are cooked.

6 Transfer the fish to warmed
serving plates and serve hot with
salad greens.

seafood pizza

serves four

5 oz/140 g standard pizza dough mix

4 tbsp chopped fresh dill, plus extra
   to garnish

SAUCE

1 large red bell pepper

14 oz/400 g canned chopped
   tomatoes with onion and herbs

3 tbsp tomato paste

salt and pepper

TOPPING

12 oz/350 g assorted cooked
   seafood, thawed if frozen

1 tbsp capers in brine, drained

1 oz/25 g pitted black olives in
   brine, drained

¼ cup grated lowfat
   mozzarella cheese

¼ cup freshly grated
   Parmesan cheese

1 Place the pizza dough mix in a
bowl and stir in the dill. Make the
dough according to the instructions
on the package.

2 Line a cookie sheet with baking
parchment. Press the herbed
pizza dough into a circle about
10 inches/25 cm wide on the prepared
cookie sheet, then leave in a warm
place to rise.

3 To make the sauce, halve and
seed the bell pepper and arrange
on a broiler rack. Cook under a
preheated broiler for 8–10 minutes,
until softened and charred. Let cool
slightly, then peel off the skin, and
chop the flesh.

4 Place the bell pepper flesh in a
pan with the canned tomatoes.
Bring to a boil, then reduce the heat,
and simmer for 10 minutes. Stir in the
tomato paste and season to taste with
salt and pepper.

5 Spread the sauce evenly over the
pizza base and top with the
seafood. Sprinkle over the capers and
olives, top with the grated cheeses,
and bake in a preheated oven, 400°F/
200°C, for 25–30 minutes. Garnish
with sprigs of fresh dill and serve hot.

COOK'S TIP

Look for packets of prepared
mixed seafood in the chiller
cabinets of large supermarkets.
These have more flavor and a
better texture than frozen.

smoked cod cornmeal

serves four

6½ cups water

generous 2⅓ cups instant cornmeal

7 oz/200 g frozen chopped spinach,
    thawed and drained

3 tbsp butter

½ cup grated romano cheese

generous ¾ cup milk

1 lb/450 g smoked cod
    fillet, skinned

4 eggs, beaten

salt and pepper

1 Bring the water to a boil in a large pan. Add the cornmeal and cook, stirring constantly, for 20–25 minutes.

2 Stir the spinach, butter, and half of the romano cheese into the cornmeal, then season to taste with salt and pepper.

3 Divide the cornmeal mixture among 4 individual ovenproof dishes, spreading it evenly across the bases and up the sides of the dishes.

4 Bring the milk to a boil in a skillet. Add the fish and simmer gently, turning once, for 8–10 minutes, until tender. Remove the fish with a slotted spoon.

5 Remove the pan from the heat. Pour the eggs into the milk in the pan and mix well together.

VARIATION

Try using 12 oz/350 g of cooked chicken breast with 2 tablespoons chopped tarragon instead of the smoked cod, if you like.

6 Using a fork, flake the fish into smaller pieces and place it in the center of the ovenproof dishes.

7 Pour the milk and egg mixture over the fish.

8 Sprinkle the remaining cheese over the top and bake in a preheated oven , 375°F/ 190°C, for 25–30 minutes, or until set and golden. Serve hot.

fillets of red snapper & pasta

serves four

2 lb 4 oz/1 kg red snapper fillets

1¼ cups dry white wine

4 shallots, chopped finely

1 garlic clove, crushed

3 tbsp finely chopped mixed
    fresh herbs

finely grated rind and juice
    of 1 lemon

pinch of freshly grated nutmeg

3 anchovy fillets, chopped coarsely

2 tbsp heavy cream

1 tsp cornstarch

1 lb/450 g dried vermicelli

1 tbsp olive oil

salt and pepper

TO GARNISH

1 fresh mint sprig

lemon slices

strips of lemon rind

2 Lift the snapper out of the casserole with a slotted spoon and transfer to a warmed dish, reserving the cooking liquid. Set the fish aside and keep warm.

3 Pour the cooking liquid into a pan and bring to a boil. Simmer for 25 minutes, until reduced by half. Mix the cream and cornstarch to a paste and stir into the sauce to thicken.

4 Meanwhile, bring a pan of lightly salted water to a boil. Add the vermicelli and oil, bring back to a boil, and cook for 8–10 minutes, until tender but still firm to the bite. Drain and transfer to a warmed serving dish.

5 Arrange the red snapper fillets on top of the vermicelli and pour over the sauce. Garnish with a sprig of fresh mint, slices of lemon, and strips of lemon rind, and serve immediately.

1 Place the red snapper fillets in a large casserole. Pour over the wine and add the shallots, garlic, herbs, lemon rind and juice, nutmeg, and anchovies. Season to taste with salt and pepper. Cover and bake in a preheated oven, 350°F/180°C, for 35 minutes.

italian chicken parcels

serves six

1 tbsp olive oil, for brushing

6 skinless, boneless chicken
   breast portions

9 oz/250 g mozzarella cheese

3½ cups sliced zucchini

6 large tomatoes, sliced

1 small bunch of fresh basil
   or oregano

pepper

rice or pasta, to serve

COOK'S TIP

To aid cooking, place the
vegetables and chicken on the
shiny side of the foil so that
when the parcel is wrapped up,
the dull surface of the foil faces
outward. The heat will be
absorbed into the parcel, and not
reflected away.

VARIATION

This recipe also works well with
monkfish fillet. Use 6 x 5–6 oz/
140–175 g fillets. Remove all the
gray membrane first.

1 Cut out 6 squares of foil, about
10-inches/25-cm wide. Brush the
squares lightly with oil and set aside.

2 Slash each chicken breast portion
3–4 times. Slice the mozzarella
cheese and tuck the slices between
the slashes.

3 Divide the zucchini and tomatoes
among the foil squares and
season with pepper. Tear or coarsely
chop the herbs and sprinkle them over
the vegetables in each parcel.

4 Place the chicken on top of each
pile of vegetables, then wrap the
foil to enclose the chicken and
vegetables, sealing at the edges.

5 Place on a cookie sheet and
bake in a preheated oven,
400°F/200°C, for about 30 minutes.

6 Unwrap each foil parcel and
serve with rice or pasta.

crispy stuffed chicken

serves four

4 skinless, boneless chicken breast
    portions, 5½ oz/150 g each

4 fresh tarragon sprigs

½ small orange bell pepper, seeded
    and sliced

½ small green bell pepper, seeded
    and sliced

¼ cup fresh whole-wheat
    bread crumbs

1 tbsp sesame seeds

4 tbsp lemon juice

salt and pepper

fresh tarragon, to garnish

BELL PEPPER SAUCE

small red bell pepper, halved
    and seeded

7 oz/200 g canned
    chopped tomatoes

1 small fresh red chile, seeded
    and chopped

¼ tsp celery salt

salt and pepper

1 Slit the chicken portion with a small, sharp knife to create a pocket in each. Season inside each pocket with salt and pepper to taste.

2 Place a sprig of tarragon and a few slices of orange and green bell pepper in each pocket. Place the chicken portions in a single layer on a nonstick cookie sheet and sprinkle the bread crumbs and sesame seeds over them.

3 Spoon 1 tablespoon of lemon juice over each chicken portion and bake in a preheated oven, 400°F/200°C, for 35–40 minutes, until the chicken is tender and cooked through.

4 Meanwhile, arrange the red bell pepper halves, skin side up, on a broiler rack, and cook under a preheated hot broiler for 5–6 minutes, until the skin starts to char and blister. Let the broiled pepper cool for 10 minutes, then peel off the skin.

5 Place the red bell pepper in a food processor, add the tomatoes, chile, and celery salt and process for a few seconds. Season to taste. Alternatively, finely chop the red bell pepper and press through a strainer with the tomatoes and chile.

6 When the chicken is cooked, heat the sauce, spoon a little onto each of 4 warmed plates, and arrange a chicken portion in the center of each. Garnish with tarragon and serve.

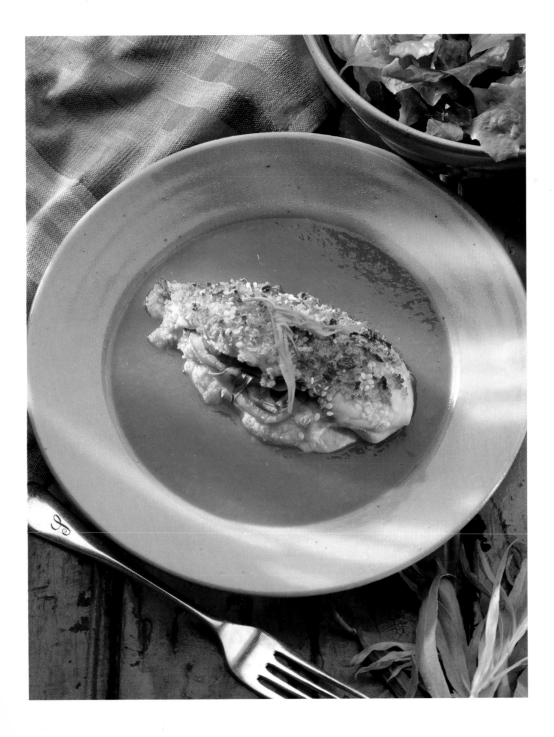

chicken & spinach lasagna

serves four

12 oz/350 g frozen chopped
spinach, thawed and drained

½ tsp ground nutmeg

1 lb/450 g lean, cooked chicken
meat, skinned and diced

4 sheets pre-cooked lasagna verde

1½ tbsp cornstarch

1¾ cups skim milk

scant ¾ cup freshly grated
Parmesan cheese

salt and pepper

TOMATO SAUCE

14 oz/400 g canned
chopped tomatoes

1 onion, chopped finely

1 garlic clove, crushed

⅔ cup white wine

3 tbsp tomato paste

1 tsp dried oregano

salt and pepper

1 To make the tomato sauce, place the tomatoes in a pan and stir in the onion, garlic, wine, tomato paste, and oregano. Bring to a boil and simmer gently for 20 minutes, stirring occasionally, until thick. Season well with salt and pepper.

2 Drain the spinach again and spread it out on paper towels to make sure that as much water as possible is removed. Layer the spinach in the base of an ovenproof dish. Sprinkle with nutmeg and season.

3 Arrange the diced chicken over the spinach and spoon over the tomato sauce. Arrange the sheets of lasagna over the tomato sauce.

4 Blend the cornstarch with a little of the milk to make a smooth paste. Pour the remaining milk into a pan and stir in the cornstarch paste. Heat gently for 2–3 minutes, stirring constantly, until the sauce thickens. Season to taste with salt and pepper.

5 Pour the sauce over the lasagna and transfer the dish to a cookie sheet. Sprinkle the Parmesan cheese over the sauce and bake in a preheated oven, 400°F/200°C, for 25 minutes, until golden brown. Serve hot.

baked chicken pasta

serves four

2 fennel bulbs

2 red onions, sliced very thinly

1 tbsp lemon juice

4½ oz/125 g white mushrooms

1 tbsp olive oil

8 oz/225 g dried penne pasta

⅓ cup raisins

8 oz/225 g lean, boneless cooked
chicken, skinned and shredded

13 oz/375 g lowfat soft cheese with
garlic and herbs

4½ oz/125 g lowfat mozzarella
cheese, sliced thinly

scant ½ cup freshly grated
Parmesan cheese

salt and pepper

1 Trim the fennel bulbs, reserving
the green fronds for the garnish,
and slice the bulbs thinly.

2 Generously coat the onions in the
lemon juice. Cut the mushrooms
into fourths.

3 Heat the oil in a large skillet and
cook the fennel, onion, and
mushrooms for 4–5 minutes, stirring,
until just softened. Season well,
transfer the mixture to a large bowl,
and set aside.

4 Bring a pan of lightly salted
water to a boil. Add the pasta,
bring back to a boil, and cook for
8–10 minutes, until tender, but still
firm to the bite. Drain and mix with
the vegetables.

5 Stir the raisins and cooked
chicken into the pasta mixture.
Beat the soft cheese to soften it
further, then mix it into the pasta and
chicken—the heat from the pasta
should make the cheese melt slightly.

6 Transfer the mixture to an
ovenproof dish and place on
a cookie sheet. Arrange slices of
mozzarella cheese over the top and
sprinkle with the Parmesan cheese.

7 Bake in a preheated oven,
400°F/200°C, for 20–25 minutes,
until golden brown.

8 Garnish with chopped fennel
fronds and serve hot.

chicken & ham lasagna

serves four

1 tbsp butter, for greasing

14 sheets pre-cooked lasagna

3½ cups Béchamel Sauce

    (see page 206)

¾ cup freshly grated

    Parmesan cheese

CHICKEN AND MUSHROOM SAUCE

2 tbsp olive oil

2 garlic cloves, crushed

1 large onion, chopped finely

8 oz/225 g exotic

    mushrooms, sliced

2½ cups ground chicken

3 oz/85 g chicken livers,

    chopped finely

¾ cup diced prosciutto

⅔ cup Marsala wine

10 oz/280 g canned

    chopped tomatoes

1 tbsp chopped fresh basil leaves

2 tbsp tomato paste

salt and pepper

1 To make the chicken and mushroom sauce, heat the olive oil in a large pan. Add the garlic, onion, and mushrooms, and cook, stirring frequently, for 6 minutes.

2 Add the ground chicken, chicken livers, and prosciutto, and cook over low heat, stirring frequently, for about 12 minutes, or until the meat has browned.

3 Stir the Marsala, tomatoes, basil, and tomato paste into the mixture and cook for 4 minutes. Season with salt and pepper, cover, and simmer for 30 minutes, stirring occasionally. Uncover the pan, stir, and simmer for 15 minutes more, uncovered.

4 Lightly grease an ovenproof dish with the butter. Arrange sheets of lasagna over the base of the dish, spoon over a layer of chicken and mushroom sauce, then spoon over a layer of béchamel sauce. Place another layer of lasagna on top and repeat the process twice, finishing with a layer of béchamel sauce. Sprinkle the grated Parmesan cheese over the top, then bake in a preheated oven, 375°F/190°C, for 35 minutes, until golden brown and bubbling. Serve immediately.

chicken lasagna

serves four

9 sheets fresh or dried lasagna

1 tbsp butter, for greasing

1 tbsp olive oil

1 red onion, chopped finely

1 garlic clove, crushed

1⅓ cups sliced mushrooms

12 oz/350 g skinless, boneless

    chicken breast portions, diced

⅔ cup red wine, diluted with a

    generous ⅓ cup water

generous 1 cup bottled

    strained tomatoes

1 tsp sugar

¾ cup freshly grated

    Parmesan cheese

salt

BÉCHAMEL SAUCE

5 tbsp butter

generous ⅓ cup all-purpose flour

2½ cups milk

1 egg, beaten

salt and pepper

1 Bring a large pan of lightly salted water to a boil. Add the lasagna and cook according to the instructions on the package. Lightly grease a deep ovenproof dish.

2 Place the oil in a pan over low heat. Add the onion and garlic and cook for 3–4 minutes. Add the mushrooms and chicken and cook for 4 minutes, or until the meat browns.

3 Add the diluted wine, bring the mixture to a boil, then reduce the heat, and simmer for 5 minutes. Stir in the tomatoes and sugar and cook for 3–5 minutes, until the meat is tender and cooked through. The sauce should have thickened, but still be quite runny.

4 To make the Béchamel Sauce, melt the butter in a pan, stir in the flour, and cook for 2 minutes, stirring constantly. Remove the pan from the heat and gradually add the milk, mixing to form a smooth sauce. Return the pan to the heat and bring to a boil, stirring until thickened. Let cool slightly, then beat in the egg and season to taste with salt and pepper. Stir half the Parmesan cheese into the béchamel sauce.

5 Place 3 sheets of lasagna in the base of the prepared dish and spread with half of the chicken mixture. Repeat the layers. Top with the last 3 sheets of lasagna, pour over the béchamel sauce, and sprinkle with the remaining Parmesan cheese. Bake in a preheated oven, 375°F/190°C, for 30 minutes, until golden and the pasta is cooked. Serve immediately.

mustard-baked chicken

serves four

4 large or 8 small chicken pieces

4 tbsp butter, melted

4 tbsp mild mustard (see Cook's Tip)

2 tbsp lemon juice

1 tbsp brown sugar

1 tsp paprika

3 tbsp poppy seeds

14 oz/400 g dried pasta shells

1 tbsp olive oil

salt and pepper

COOK'S TIP

Dijon is the type of mustard most often used in cooking, as it has a clean and mildly spicy flavor, compared to American mustard, which is mild and sweet. German mustard has a sweet-sour taste, although Bavarian mustard is slightly sweeter.

VARIATION

This recipe would also work well with a variety of feathered game, such as guinea fowl and young pheasant.

1 Arrange the chicken pieces in a single layer in the base of a large ovenproof dish.

2 Combine the butter, mustard, lemon juice, sugar, and paprika in a bowl and season with salt and pepper to taste. Brush the mixture over the upper surfaces of the chicken pieces and bake in a preheated oven, 400°F/200°C, for 15 minutes.

3 Remove the dish from the oven and carefully turn over the chicken. Coat the upper surfaces of the chicken pieces with the remaining mustard mixture, sprinkle over the poppy seeds, and return to the oven for 15 minutes more.

4 Meanwhile, bring a large pan of lightly salted water to a boil. Add the pasta shells and olive oil, bring back to a boil, and cook for about 8–10 minutes, or until tender but still firm to the bite.

5 Drain the pasta thoroughly and arrange on 4 warmed serving plates. Top the pasta with the chicken pieces, pour over the mustard sauce, and serve immediately.

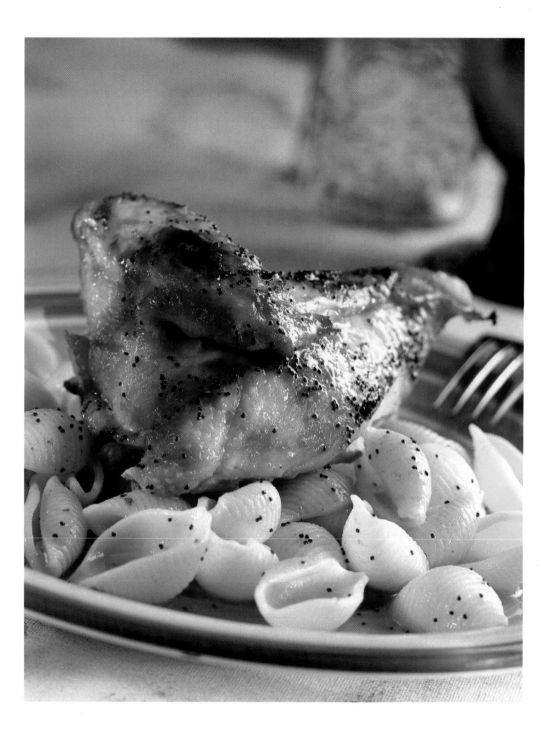

roast duckling with apple

serves four

4 duckling pieces, about
    12 oz/350 g each

4 tbsp dark soy sauce

2 tbsp light brown sugar

2 red-skinned apples

2 green-skinned apples

juice of 1 lemon

2 tbsp honey

a few bay leaves

salt and pepper

a selection of fresh vegetables,
    to serve

APRICOT SAUCE

14 oz/400 g canned apricots,
    in natural juice

4 tbsp sweet sherry

1 Wash the duckling and trim off any excess fat. Place on a wire rack over a roasting pan and prick all over with a fork.

2 Brush the duck with the soy sauce. Sprinkle over the brown sugar and season with pepper. Cook in a preheated oven, 375°F/190°C, basting occasionally, for about 50–60 minutes, until the meat is cooked through—the juices should run clear when a skewer is inserted into the thickest part of the meat.

3 Meanwhile, core the apples and cut each of them into 6 wedges. Mix with the lemon juice and honey in a bowl. Place the fruit and liquid in a

small roasting pan. Add a few bay leaves and season. Cook alongside the duckling, basting occasionally, for 20–25 minutes, until tender. Discard the bay leaves.

4 To make the sauce, place the apricots and their juices in a blender or food processor with the sherry, then process into a paste. Alternatively, mash the apricots with a fork, then mix in the juice and sherry.

5 Just before serving, heat the apricot sauce in a small pan. Remove the skin from the duckling and pat the flesh with paper towels to absorb any fat. Serve the duckling with the apple wedges, apricot sauce, and fresh vegetables.

pesto-baked partridge

serves four

8 partridge pieces, 115 g/4 oz each

4 tbsp butter, melted

4 tbsp Dijon mustard

2 tbsp lime juice

1 tbsp brown sugar

6 tbsp Pesto Sauce (see page 7)

1 lb/450 g dried rigatoni pasta

1 tbsp olive oil

1 cup freshly grated
   Parmesan cheese

salt and pepper

VARIATION
You could also prepare young
pheasant in the same way.

1 Arrange the partridge pieces,
smooth side down, in a single
layer in a large, ovenproof dish.

2 Combine the butter, Dijon
mustard, lime juice, and brown
sugar in a bowl. Season to taste with
salt and pepper. Brush the mixture
over the partridge pieces, reserving
the remaining mixture, and bake in a
preheated oven, 400°F/200°C, for
15 minutes.

3 Remove the dish from the oven
and coat the partridge pieces
with 3 tablespoons of the pesto sauce.
Return the dish to the oven and bake
for 12 minutes more.

4 Remove the dish from the oven
and carefully turn over the
partridge pieces. Coat the top of the
partridge with the remaining mustard
mixture and return to the oven for
another 10 minutes.

5 Meanwhile, bring a large pan of
lightly salted water to a boil. Add
the rigatoni and olive oil, bring back to
a boil, and cook for 8–10 minutes,
until tender but still firm to the bite.
Drain and transfer to a serving dish.

6 Add the remaining pesto sauce
and the Parmesan cheese to the
pasta and toss thoroughly to blend.
Transfer the partridge to serving plates
and serve with the pasta, pouring over
the cooking juices.

honey-glazed duck

serves four

2 large, boneless duck breasts,
about 8 oz/225 g each

MARINADE

1 tsp dark soy sauce

2 tbsp honey

1 tsp garlic vinegar

2 garlic cloves, crushed

1 tsp ground star anise

2 tsp cornstarch

2 tsp water

TO GARNISH

celery leaves

cucumber wedges

fresh chives

COOK'S TIP

If the duck begins to burn
slightly while it is cooking, cover
with foil. Check that the duck
breasts are cooked through by
inserting the point of a sharp
knife into the thickest part of the
meat—the juices should run
clear when the duck is cooked.

1 To make the marinade, combine
the soy sauce, honey, garlic
vinegar, garlic, and star anise in a
bowl. Blend the cornstarch with the
water to form a smooth paste and stir
it into the mixture.

2 Place the duck in a shallow dish.
Brush the marinade over the
duck, turning the meat to coat. Cover
and marinate in the refrigerator for at
least 2 hours, or overnight.

3 Drain the duck, reserving the
marinade. Place in a shallow
ovenproof dish and bake in a
preheated oven, 425°F/220°C, for
20–25 minutes, basting frequently
with the marinade.

4 Remove the duck from the oven
and transfer to a preheated
medium broiler. Broil for 3–4 minutes
to caramelize the top.

5 Remove the duck from the broiler
rack and cut into fairly thin slices.
Arrange the slices on a warmed
serving dish, garnish with celery
leaves, cucumber wedges, and fresh
chives, and serve immediately.

red roast pork in soy sauce

serves four

1 lb/450 g lean pork tenderloin

MARINADE

6 tbsp dark soy sauce

2 tbsp dry sherry

1 tsp Chinese five-spice powder

2 garlic cloves, crushed

2 tsp finely chopped fresh gingerroot

1 large red bell pepper

1 large yellow bell pepper

1 large orange bell pepper

4 tbsp superfine sugar

2 tbsp red wine vinegar

TO GARNISH

shredded scallions

snipped fresh chives

1 Trim away any excess fat and the silver skin from the pork and place in a shallow dish.

2 To make the marinade, mix the soy sauce, sherry, five-spice powder, garlic, and ginger together in a bowl. Spoon over the pork, turning it to coat, cover, and marinate in the refrigerator for at least 1 hour, or until required.

3 Drain the pork, reserving the marinade. Place the pork on a roasting rack over a roasting pan. Cook in a preheated oven, 375°F/190°C, basting occasionally with the marinade, for 1 hour, or until cooked through.

4 Meanwhile, halve and seed the bell peppers. Cut each bell pepper half into 3 equal portions. Arrange them on a cookie sheet and bake alongside the pork for the last 30 minutes of cooking time.

5 Place the sugar and vinegar in a pan and heat gently until the sugar dissolves. Bring to a boil and simmer for 3–4 minutes, until syrupy.

6 When the pork is cooked, remove it from the oven and brush with the sugar syrup. Let stand for about 5 minutes, then slice, and arrange on a warmed serving plate. Garnish with scallions and freshly snipped chives and serve.

braised fennel & linguine

serves four

6 fennel bulbs

⅔ cup Vegetable Bouillon
   (see page 7)

2 tbsp butter

6 strips lean smoked
   bacon, diced

6 shallots, cut into fourths

¼ cup all-purpose flour

scant ½ cup heavy cream

1 tbsp Madeira

1 lb/450 g dried linguine pasta

1 tbsp olive oil

salt and pepper

1 Trim the fennel bulbs, then peel off and reserve the outer layer of each. Cut the bulbs into quarters and put them in a large pan with the bouillon and the reserved outer layers.

2 Bring to a boil, lower the heat, and simmer for 5 minutes.

3 Using a slotted spoon, transfer the fennel to a large dish, discarding the outer layers of the bulbs. Bring the bouillon to a boil and reduce by half. Set aside.

4 Melt the butter in a skillet over low heat. Add the bacon and shallots and cook, stirring occasionally, for 4 minutes. Add the flour, reduced

bouillon, cream, and Madeira and cook, stirring constantly, for 3 minutes, or until the sauce is smooth. Season to taste with salt and pepper and pour over the fennel.

5 Bring a pan of lightly salted water to a boil. Add the pasta and oil, bring back to a boil, and cook for 8–10 minutes, or until tender but still firm to the bite. Drain, and transfer to an ovenproof dish.

6 Add the fennel and the sauce and braise in a preheated oven, 350°F/180°C, for 20 minutes, until the fennel is tender. Serve immediately.

stuffed cannelloni

serves four

8 dried cannelloni tubes

1 tbsp olive oil

⅓ cup freshly grated
    Parmesan cheese

fresh flatleaf parsley sprigs,
    to garnish

FILLING

2 tbsp butter

10½ oz/300 g frozen chopped
    spinach, thawed and drained

½ cup ricotta cheese

⅓ cup freshly grated
    Parmesan cheese

¼ cup chopped ham

pinch of freshly grated nutmeg

2 tbsp heavy cream

2 eggs, lightly beaten

salt and pepper

SAUCE

2 tbsp butter

scant ¼ cup all-purpose flour

1¼ cups milk

2 bay leaves

pinch of freshly grated nutmeg

salt and pepper

1 To make the filling, melt the butter in a pan, add the spinach, and cook for 2–3 minutes. Remove from the heat, transfer to an ovenproof bowl, and stir in the ricotta, Parmesan cheese, and ham. Season to taste with nutmeg, salt, and pepper. Beat in the cream and eggs to make a thick paste.

2 Bring a pan of lightly salted water to a boil. Add the cannelloni and the oil, return to a boil, and cook for 10–12 minutes, or until tender but still firm to the bite. Drain and let cool.

3 To make the sauce, melt the butter in a pan. Stir in the flour and cook, stirring, for 1 minute. Gradually stir in the milk. Add the bay leaves and simmer, stirring, for 5 minutes. Add the nutmeg and salt and pepper to taste. Remove from the heat and discard the bay leaves.

4 Spoon the filling into a pastry bag and fill the cooked cannelloni.

5 Spoon a little sauce into the base of an ovenproof dish. Arrange the cannelloni in the dish in a single layer and pour over the remaining sauce. Sprinkle over the Parmesan cheese and bake in a preheated oven, 375°F/190°C, for 40–45 minutes. Garnish with sprigs of fresh flatleaf parsley and serve immediately.

italian calzone

serves four

1 quantity Basic Pizza Dough
  (see page 6)
1 egg, beaten
FILLING
1 tbsp tomato paste
1 oz/25 g Italian salami, chopped
1 oz/25 g mortadella, chopped
1 tomato, peeled and chopped
2 tbsp ricotta cheese
2 scallions, trimmed and chopped
¼ tsp dried oregano
salt and pepper
fresh flatleaf parsley, to garnish

1 Knead the Basic Pizza Dough and roll out on a lightly floured counter into a 9-inch/23-cm circle.

2 Brush the edge of the dough with a little beaten egg. Reserve the remaining egg.

3 Spread the tomato paste over the half of the circle nearest to you.

4 Sprinkle the salami, mortadella, and chopped tomato on top.

5 Dot with the ricotta cheese and then evenly sprinkle over the scallions and oregano. Season to taste.

6 Fold over the other half of the dough to form a semicircle shape. Press the edges together well to prevent the filling from leaking out.

7 Place the calzone on a cookie sheet and brush with beaten egg to glaze. Make a small hole in the top with a knife to allow steam to escape during cooking.

8 Bake in a preheated oven, 400°F/ 200°C, for 20 minutes, or until golden. Transfer to a warmed serving plate, garnish with flatleaf parsley, and serve immediately.

eggplant pasta cake

serves four

1 tbsp butter, for greasing

1 eggplant

10½ oz/300 g dried tricolor
    pasta shapes

½ cup lowfat soft cheese with garlic
    and herbs

1½ cups bottled strained tomatoes

scant ¾ cup freshly grated
    Parmesan cheese

1½ tsp dried oregano

2 tbsp dry white bread crumbs

salt and pepper

fresh oregano sprigs, to garnish

1 Grease an 8-inch/20-cm round springform cake pan and line it with baking parchment.

2 Trim the eggplant. Cut lengthwise into slices about ¼ inch/5 mm thick. Place in a bowl and sprinkle with salt, then let stand for 30 minutes, to remove any bitter juices. Rinse well under cold running water and drain.

3 Bring a pan of water to a boil and blanch the eggplant slices for 1 minute. Drain and pat dry with paper towels. Set aside.

4 Bring a separate large pan of lightly salted water to a boil. Add the pasta shapes, bring back to a boil, and cook for 8–10 minutes, until tender but still firm to the bite. Drain well and return to the pan. Add the lowfat soft cheese and let it melt over the pasta.

5 Stir in the tomatoes, Parmesan cheese, and oregano, and season to taste with salt and pepper. Set aside.

6 Arrange the eggplant slices over the base and sides of the cake pan, overlapping them and making sure there are no gaps.

7 Pile the pasta mixture into the pan, packing it down well, and sprinkle with the bread crumbs. Bake in

a preheated oven, 375°F/190°C, for 20 minutes. Remove from the oven and let stand for 15 minutes.

8 Loosen the cake around the edge of the pan with a spatula, and turn it out, eggplant side uppermost. Garnish with fresh oregano and serve.

pasticcio

serves six

8 oz/225 g dried fusilli, or other
   short pasta shapes
1 tbsp olive oil, plus extra
   for brushing
4 tbsp heavy cream
salt
fresh rosemary sprigs, to garnish
BEEF SAUCE
2 tbsp olive oil
1 onion, thinly sliced
1 red bell pepper, seeded
   and chopped
2 garlic cloves, chopped
1 lb 6 oz/625 g lean ground beef
14 oz/400 g canned
   chopped tomatoes
½ cup dry white wine
2 tbsp chopped fresh parsley
1¾ oz/50 g canned anchovies,
   drained and chopped
salt and pepper
TOPPING
1¼ cups plain yogurt
3 eggs
pinch of freshly grated nutmeg
½ cup freshly grated
   Parmesan cheese
salt and pepper

1 To make the sauce, heat the oil in a large skillet, add the onion and red bell pepper, and cook for 3 minutes. Stir in the garlic and cook for 1 minute. Stir in the beef and cook, stirring frequently, until browned.

2 Add the tomatoes and wine, stir, and bring to a boil. Simmer, uncovered, for 20 minutes, or until the sauce is fairly thick. Stir in the parsley and anchovies and season to taste.

3 Bring a large pan of lightly salted water to a boil. Add the pasta and olive oil, return to a boil, and cook for 8–10 minutes, until tender but still firm to the bite. Drain, then transfer to a bowl. Stir in the cream and set aside.

4 To make the topping, beat together the yogurt, eggs, and nutmeg until well blended, and season with salt and pepper, to taste.

5 Brush a large, shallow ovenproof dish with oil. Spoon in half of the pasta mixture and cover with half of the beef sauce. Repeat the layers, then spread the topping evenly over the final layer. Sprinkle the grated Parmesan cheese on top.

6 Bake in a preheated oven, 375°F/ 190°C, for 25 minutes, or until the topping is golden brown and bubbling. Garnish with sprigs of fresh rosemary and serve.

hot pot chops

serves four

4 lean, boneless lamb leg steaks,
    about 4½ oz/125 g each

1 small onion, sliced thinly

1 carrot, sliced thinly

1 potato, sliced thinly

1 tsp olive oil

1 tsp dried rosemary

salt and pepper

fresh rosemary, to garnish

freshly steamed green vegetables,
    to serve

1 Trim any excess fat from the lamb steaks using a sharp knife.

2 Season both sides of the steaks with salt and pepper to taste and arrange them on a cookie sheet.

3 Alternate layers of sliced onion, carrot, and potato on top of each lamb steak, finishing with a layer of potato on top.

4 Brush the top layer of potato lightly with oil, season with salt and pepper to taste, then sprinkle with a little dried rosemary.

5 Bake the hot pot chops in a preheated oven, 350°F./180°C, for 25–30 minutes, until the lamb is tender and cooked through.

6 Drain the lamb steaks on paper towels and transfer to a warmed serving plate.

7 Garnish with fresh rosemary and serve accompanied by freshly steamed green vegetables.

fruity lamb casserole

serves four

1 lb/450 g lean lamb, trimmed and
    cut into 1-inch/2.5-cm cubes

1 tsp ground cinnamon

1 tsp ground coriander

1 tsp ground cumin

2 tsp olive oil

1 red onion, chopped finely

1 garlic clove, crushed

14 oz/400 g canned
    chopped tomatoes

2 tbsp tomato paste

4½ oz/125 g no-soak dried apricots

1 tsp superfine sugar

1¼ cups Vegetable Bouillon
    (see page 7)

salt and pepper

1 small bunch of fresh cilantro,
    to garnish

rice or couscous, to serve

1 Place the lamb in a mixing bowl and add the cinnamon, coriander, cumin, and oil. Mix thoroughly to coat the lamb in the spices.

2 Place a nonstick skillet over a high heat for a few seconds until hot, then add the spiced lamb. Reduce the heat and cook for 4–5 minutes, stirring, until the meat has browned all over. Remove the lamb using a slotted spoon and transfer to a large casserole.

3 Add the onion, garlic, tomatoes, and tomato paste to the skillet and cook, stirring occasionally, for 5 minutes. Season to taste with salt and pepper. Stir in the dried apricots and sugar, add the bouillon, and bring to a boil.

4 Spoon the sauce over the lamb and mix well. Cover and cook in a preheated oven, 350°F/180°C, for 1 hour, removing the lid for the last 10 minutes.

5 Chop the cilantro and use it to garnish the lamb. Serve immediately, straight from the casserole, with rice or couscous.

223

fresh spaghetti & meatballs

serves four

2½ cups fresh whole-wheat
   bread crumbs

⅔ cup milk

1 large onion, chopped

4 cups ground steak

1 tsp paprika

4 tbsp olive oil

1 tbsp butter

1 lb/450 g fresh spaghetti

salt and pepper

fresh tarragon sprigs, to garnish

TOMATO SAUCE

1 tbsp butter

¼ cup whole-wheat flour

generous ¾ cup beef bouillon

14 oz/400 g canned
   chopped tomatoes

2 tbsp tomato paste

1 tsp sugar

1 tbsp finely chopped fresh tarragon

salt and pepper

1 Place the bread crumbs in a bowl, add the milk, and soak for about 30 minutes.

2 To make the tomato sauce, melt half of the butter in a pan. Add the flour and cook, stirring constantly, for 2 minutes. Gradually stir in the beef bouillon and cook, stirring, for 5 minutes more. Add the tomatoes, tomato paste, sugar, and tarragon. Season and simmer for 25 minutes.

3 Mix the onion, steak, and paprika into the bread crumbs and season to taste with salt and pepper. Shape the mixture into 14 meatballs.

4 Heat the oil and butter in a skillet over low heat, add the meatballs, and cook, turning, until browned all over. Place the meatballs in a deep casserole, pour over the tomato sauce, cover, and bake in a preheated oven, 350°F/180°C, for 25 minutes.

5 Bring a large pan of lightly salted water to a boil. Add the fresh spaghetti, bring back to a boil, and cook for about 2–3 minutes, or until tender but still firm to the bite.

6 Meanwhile, remove the meatballs from the oven and let cool for 3 minutes. Drain the spaghetti and transfer to a serving dish, then pour the meatballs and their sauce over the top. Garnish with tarragon and serve.

meatballs in red wine sauce

serves four

generous 2½ cups fresh white
   bread crumbs

⅔ cup milk

12 shallots, chopped

4 cups ground steak

1 tsp paprika

5 tbsp olive oil

1 tbsp butter

1 lb/450 g dried egg tagliatelle

salt and pepper

fresh basil sprigs, to garnish

MUSHROOM AND WINE SAUCE

1 tbsp butter

4 tbsp olive oil

3 cups sliced oyster mushrooms

¼ cup whole-wheat flour

generous ¾ cup beef bouillon

⅔ cup red wine

4 tomatoes, peeled and chopped

1 tbsp tomato paste

1 tsp brown sugar

1 tbsp finely chopped fresh basil

salt and pepper

1 Place the bread crumbs in a bowl, add the milk, and let soak for 30 minutes.

2 To make the sauce, heat half of the butter and the oil in a large pan. Add the mushrooms and cook for 4 minutes. Stir in the flour and cook for 2 minutes. Add the bouillon and wine and simmer for 15 minutes. Add the tomatoes, tomato paste, sugar, basil, and seasoning. Simmer for 30 minutes.

3 Mix the shallots, steak, and paprika with the bread crumbs and season to taste with salt and pepper. Shape the mixture into 14 meatballs.

4 Heat 4 tablespoons of the oil and the butter in a large skillet over medium heat. Add the meatballs and cook, turning frequently, until browned all over. Transfer the meatballs to a deep casserole and pour over the wine and mushroom sauce. Cover, and bake in a preheated oven, 350°F/180°C, for 30 minutes.

5 Bring a pan of lightly salted water to a boil. Add the pasta and the remaining oil, bring back to a boil, and cook for 8–10 minutes, or until tender but still firm to the bite. Drain and transfer to a serving dish.

6 Remove the casserole from the oven and let cool for 3 minutes. Pour the meatballs and sauce over the pasta, garnish with sprigs of basil, and serve.

lasagna verde

serves six

Ragù Sauce (see page 6)

1 tbsp olive oil

8 oz/225 g lasagna verde

1 tbsp butter, for greasing

Béchamel Sauce (see page 206)

²/₃ cup freshly grated
  Parmesan cheese

salt and pepper

salad greens, tomato salad, or black
  olives, to serve

1 First, make the ragù sauce as described on page 6, but cook for 10–12 minutes longer than the time given, uncovered, to let the excess liquid evaporate. The sauce needs to be reduced to a thick paste.

2 Bring a large pan of lightly salted, water to a boil and add the olive oil. Drop the lasagna sheets into the boiling water, a few at a time, bringing back to a boil before adding further sheets. If you are using fresh lasagna sheets, cook them for about 8 minutes; if you are using dried lasagna sheets or partly pre-cooked lasagna sheets, cook them according to the instructions on the package.

3 Remove the lasagna sheets from the pan with a slotted spoon. Spread them out in a single layer on clean, damp dish towels.

4 Grease a rectangular ovenproof dish measuring 10–11 inches/ 25–28 cm long. Spoon a little of the meat sauce into the base of the prepared dish, cover with a layer of lasagna, then spoon over a little of the béchamel sauce, and sprinkle with some of the Parmesan cheese. Repeat the layers, covering the final layer of lasagna sheets with the remaining béchamel sauce.

5 Sprinkle over the remaining cheese and bake in a preheated oven, 375°F/190°C, for 40 minutes, or until the sauce is golden brown and bubbling. Serve with salad greens, a tomato salad, or a bowl of black olives.

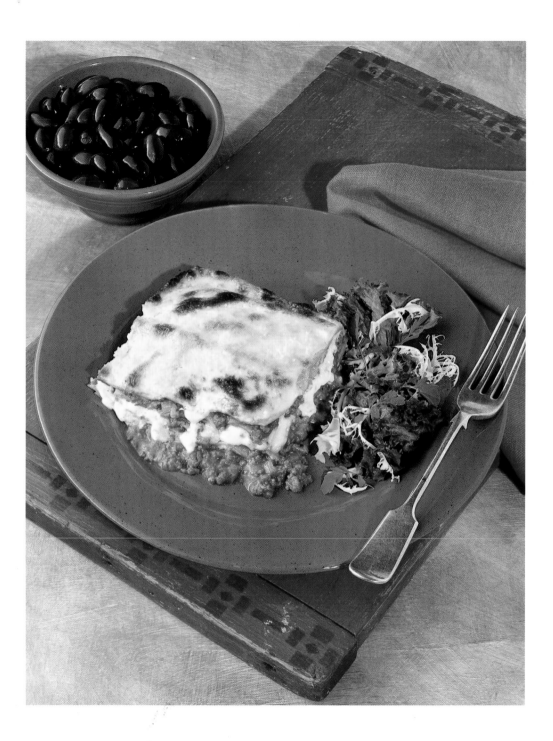

beef & pasta casserole

serves four

2 lb/900 g steak, cubed

⅔ cup beef bouillon

1 lb/450 g dried macaroni

1¼ cups heavy cream

½ tsp garam masala

salt

KORMA PASTE

½ cup blanched almonds

6 garlic cloves

3 tsp coarsely chopped
   fresh gingerroot

6 tbsp beef bouillon

1 tsp ground cardamom

4 cloves, crushed

1 tsp cinnamon

2 large onions, chopped

1 tsp coriander seeds

2 tsp ground cumin seeds

pinch of cayenne pepper

6 tbsp sunflower oil

TO GARNISH

fresh cilantro

sliced almonds

1 To make the korma paste, grind the blanched almonds finely using a pestle and mortar. Put the ground almonds and the rest of the korma paste ingredients into a food processor and process to a very smooth paste.

2 Put the steak in a shallow dish and spoon over the korma paste, turning the steak to coat thoroughly. Set the meat aside in the refrigerator to marinate for 6 hours.

3 Transfer the steak and korma paste to a large pan and simmer over low heat, adding a little beef bouillon if required, for 35 minutes.

4 Meanwhile, bring a large pan of lightly salted water to a boil. Add the macaroni, bring back to a boil, and cook for 10 minutes, until tender but still firm to the bite. Drain the pasta thoroughly and transfer to a deep casserole. Add the steak, cream, and garam masala.

5 Bake in a preheated oven, 400°F/ 200°C, for 30 minutes, until the steak is tender. Remove from the oven and let stand for 10 minutes. Garnish the casserole with cilantro and sliced almonds and serve hot.

neopolitan veal cutlets

serves four

¾ cup butter

4 veal cutlets, about 9 oz/250 g
  each, trimmed

1 large onion, sliced

2 apples, peeled, cored, and sliced

6 oz/175 g white mushrooms

1 tbsp chopped fresh tarragon

8 black peppercorns

1 tbsp sesame seeds

2 large beefsteak tomatoes,
  cut in half

leaves of 1 fresh basil sprig

14 oz/400 g dried marille pasta

scant ½ cup extra virgin olive oil

¾ cup mascarpone cheese

salt and pepper

fresh basil leaves, to garnish

1 Melt ¼ cup of the butter in a skillet. Add the veal and cook over low heat for 5 minutes on each side. Transfer to a dish and keep warm.

2 Add the onion and apple slices to the skillet and cook, stirring occasionally, for 5–8 minutes, until lightly browned. Transfer to an ovenproof dish, place the veal on top, and keep warm.

3 Melt all but 1 tablespoon of the remaining butter in the skillet. Add the mushrooms, tarragon, and peppercorns. Cook over low heat for 3 minutes. Stir in the sesame seeds and transfer to a bowl with the pan juices. Set aside. Add the tomatoes and basil to the pan with the remaining butter, cook for 2–3 minutes. Set aside.

4 Bring a large pan of lightly salted water to a boil. Add the pasta and 1 tablespoon of the oil, bring back to a boil, and cook for 8–10 minutes, or until tender but still firm to the bite.

Drain well and transfer to an ovenproof dish. Dot with the mascarpone and sprinkle over the remaining olive oil.

5 Place the onions, apples, and veal on top of the pasta. Spoon the mushroom mixture onto the cutlets with the pan juices, place the tomatoes and basil leaves around the edge, and bake in a preheated oven, 300°F/ 150°C, for 5 minutes.

6 Remove from the oven and transfer to serving plates. Season, garnish with basil, and serve.

Vegetarian & Vegan

Anyone who ever thought that vegetarian meals were dull will be proved wrong by the rich variety of dishes in this chapter. You'll recognize influences from Middle Eastern and Italian cooking, such as the Stuffed Vegetables, Roasted Bell Pepper Bread, and Sun-dried Tomato Loaf, but there are also traditional recipes such as Pineapple Upside-Down Cake and Fruit Crumble. They all make exciting treats at any time of year and for virtually any occasion. Don't be afraid to substitute some of your own personal favorite ingredients wherever appropriate.

spicy black-eyed peas

serves four

2 cups black-eyed peas, soaked
overnight in cold water

1 tbsp vegetable oil

2 onions, chopped

1 tbsp honey

2 tbsp molasses

4 tbsp dark soy sauce

1 tsp dry mustard powder

4 tbsp tomato paste

scant 2 cups Vegetable Bouillon
(see page 7)

1 bay leaf

1 each fresh rosemary, thyme,
and sage sprig

1 small orange

1 tbsp cornstarch

2 red bell peppers, seeded
and diced

pepper

2 tbsp chopped fresh flatleaf
parsley, to garnish

crusty bread, to serve

1 Rinse the black-eyed peas and place in a pan. Cover with water, bring to a boil, and boil rapidly for 10 minutes. Drain the peas and place in a casserole.

2 Meanwhile, heat the oil in a large skillet, add the onions, and cook over low heat, stirring occasionally, for 5 minutes. Stir in the honey, molasses, soy sauce, mustard, and tomato paste. Pour in the bouillon, bring to a boil, and pour over the peas.

3 Tie the bay leaf and herbs together with a clean piece of string and add to the pea mixture in the casserole. Finely pare 3 pieces of orange rind using a swivel vegetable peeler and stir into the pea mixture, with plenty of pepper. Cover and cook in a preheated oven, 300°F/150°C, for 1 hour.

4 Extract the juice from the orange and blend with the cornstarch to form a paste. Remove the casserole from the oven and stir the cornstarch paste into the peas with the red bell peppers. Cover, return to the oven, and cook for 1 hour, until the sauce is rich and thick and the peas are tender. Discard the herbs and orange rind.

5 Garnish the casserole with chopped flatleaf parsley and serve with crusty bread.

pasta & bean casserole

serves six

generous 1 cup dried navy beans,
    soaked overnight and drained

6 tbsp olive oil

2 large onions, sliced

2 garlic cloves, chopped

2 bay leaves

1 tsp dried oregano

1 tsp dried thyme

5 tbsp red wine

2 tbsp tomato paste

3½ cups Vegetable Bouillon
    (see page 7)

8 oz/225 g dried penne, or other
    short pasta shapes

2 celery stalks, sliced

1 fennel bulb, sliced

scant 2 cups sliced mushrooms

8 oz/225 g tomatoes, sliced

1 tsp dark molasses sugar

scant 1 cup dry white bread crumbs

salt and pepper

TO SERVE

salad greens

crusty bread

1 Place the beans in a pan, cover with water, and bring to a boil. Boil rapidly for 20 minutes, then drain.

2 Place the beans in a large flameproof casserole, stir in 5 tablespoons of the olive oil, the onions, garlic, bay leaves, herbs, wine, and tomato paste, and pour in the vegetable bouillon.

3 Bring to a boil, then cover the casserole, and bake in a preheated oven, 350°F/180°C, for 2 hours.

4 Towards the end of the cooking time, bring a large pan of salted water to the boil, add the pasta and the remaining olive oil and cook for 3 minutes. Drain and set aside.

5 Remove the casserole from the oven and add the pasta, celery, fennel, mushrooms, and tomatoes, and season to taste with salt and pepper.

6 Stir in the sugar and sprinkle over the bread crumbs. Cover the casserole, return to the oven, and continue cooking for 1 hour. Serve hot with salad greens and crusty bread.

mushroom cannelloni

serves four

12 oz/350 g crimini mushrooms

1 onion, chopped finely

1 garlic clove, crushed

1 tbsp chopped fresh thyme

½ tsp ground nutmeg

4 tbsp dry white wine

scant 1 cup fresh white
    bread crumbs

12 dried quick-cook cannelloni

salt and pepper

Parmesan shavings, to garnish

TOMATO SAUCE

1 large red bell pepper

¾ cup dry white wine

scant 2 cups bottled
    strained tomatoes

2 tbsp tomato paste

2 bay leaves

1 tsp superfine sugar

1 Finely chop the mushrooms and place in a pan with the onion and garlic. Stir in the thyme, nutmeg, and wine. Bring to a boil, cover, and simmer for 10 minutes.

2 Add the bread crumbs, stir to bind the mixture together, and season to taste. Remove from the heat and let cool for 10 minutes.

3 To make the tomato sauce, cut the bell pepper in half, seed it, and place on the broiler rack. Cook under a preheated hot broiler for 8–10 minutes, until charred. Let cool.

4 When the bell pepper has cooled, peel off the charred skin. Chop the flesh and place in a food processor with the wine. Process into a paste, then pour into a pan.

5 Add the remaining sauce ingredients to the paste and stir. Bring to a boil and simmer for 10 minutes. Discard the bay leaves.

6 Cover the base of an ovenproof dish with a thin layer of tomato sauce. Fill the cannelloni with the mushroom mixture and place in the dish. Spoon over the remaining sauce, cover with foil, and bake in a preheated oven, 400°F/200°C, for 35–40 minutes. Garnish with Parmesan shavings and serve.

stuffed vegetables

serves four

4 large beefsteak tomatoes

4 zucchini

2 orange bell peppers

salt and pepper

FILLING

1¼ cups cracked wheat

¼ cucumber

1 red onion

2 tbsp lemon juice

2 tbsp chopped fresh cilantro

2 tbsp chopped fresh mint

1 tbsp olive oil

2 tsp cumin seeds

salt and pepper

TO SERVE

warm pita bread

hummus

COOK'S TIP

It is a good idea to blanch vegetables (except for tomatoes) before stuffing. Blanch bell peppers, zucchini, and eggplant for 5 minutes.

1 Slice the tops off the tomatoes and reserve, then scoop out the tomato pulp. Chop the pulp and place in a bowl. Season the tomato shells with salt and pepper, then invert them on absorbent paper towels, and set aside to drain.

2 Trim the zucchini and cut a V-shaped groove lengthwise down each one. Finely chop the cut-out wedges and add to the tomato pulp. Season the zucchini shells to taste and set aside. Halve the bell peppers, cutting carefully through the stalks. Cut out the seeds and discard, leaving the stalks intact. Season the bell pepper shells and set aside.

3 To make the filling, soak the cracked wheat according to the instructions on the package. Finely chop the cucumber and add to the reserved tomato pulp and zucchini mixture. Finely chop the red onion and add to the vegetable mixture with the lemon juice, herbs, olive oil, cumin, and seasoning, and mix together well.

4 When the wheat has soaked, mix with the vegetables, and stuff into the tomato, zucchini, and bell pepper shells. Place the tops on the tomatoes, transfer to a roasting pan, and bake in a preheated oven, 400°F/ 200°C, for about 20–25 minutes, until cooked through. Drain and serve with pita bread and hummus.

lentil & red bell pepper tart

serves six

DOUGH

1¾ cups plain whole-wheat flour,
   plus extra for dusting

⅓ cup vegan margarine, diced

4 tbsp water

FILLING

¾ cup red lentils, rinsed

1¼ cups Vegetable Bouillon
   (see page 7)

1 tbsp vegan margarine

1 onion, chopped

2 red bell peppers, seeded
   and diced

1 tsp yeast extract

1 tbsp tomato paste

3 tbsp chopped fresh parsley

pepper

1 To make the dough, strain the flour into a mixing bowl and add any bran remaining in the strainer. Rub in the vegan margarine with your fingertips until the mixture resembles fine bread crumbs. Stir in the water and bring together to form a dough. Wrap in plastic wrap and chill in the refrigerator for 30 minutes.

2 Meanwhile, to make the filling, put the lentils in a pan with the stick, bring to a boil, then simmer for 10 minutes, until the lentils are tender. Remove from the heat and mash the lentils into a paste.

3 Melt the margarine in a small skillet over low heat, add the onion and red bell peppers and cook for about 3 minutes, stirring occasionally, until just soft.

4 Add the lentil paste, yeast extract, tomato paste, and parsley. Season with pepper. Mix until well blended.

5 Roll out the dough on a lightly floured counter and use it to line a 9½-inch/24-cm loose-based tart pan. Prick the base of the tart shell with a fork and spoon the lentil mixture into the shell.

6 Bake in a preheated oven, 400°F/ 200°C, for 30 minutes, until the filling is set. Serve immediately.

brazil nut & mushroom pie

serves four

DOUGH

1¾ cups plain whole-
  wheat flour

⅓ cup vegan margarine, diced

4 tbsp water

soy milk, to glaze

FILLING

2 tbsp vegan margarine

1 onion, chopped

1 garlic clove, chopped finely

scant 2 cups sliced
  white mushrooms

1 tbsp all-purpose flour

⅔ cup Vegetable Stock
  (see page 7)

1 tbsp tomato paste

generous 1 cup chopped Brazil nuts

1⅔ cup fresh whole-wheat
  bread crumbs

2 tbsp chopped fresh parsley

½ tsp pepper

1 To make the dough, strain the flour into a mixing bowl and add any bran remaining in the strainer. Rub in the vegan margarine with your fingertips until the mixture resembles fine bread crumbs. Stir in the water and bring together to form a dough. Wrap in plastic wrap and chill in the refrigerator for 30 minutes.

2 Meanwhile, to make the filling, melt half of the margarine in a skillet over low heat. Add the onion, garlic, and mushrooms and cook, stirring occasionally, for 5 minutes, until softened. Add the flour and cook for 1 minute, stirring constantly. Gradually add the bouillon, stirring, until the sauce is smooth and starting to thicken. Stir in the tomato paste, Brazil nuts, bread crumbs, parsley, and pepper. Remove the pan from the heat and let cool slightly.

3 Roll out two-thirds of the dough on a lightly floured counter and use it to line an 8-inch/20-cm loose-based tart pan or pie dish. Spread the filling in the pie shell. Brush the edges of the dough with soy milk. Roll out the remaining dough to fit the top of the pie. Press the edges to seal, then make a slit in the top of the pie to let steam escape during cooking, and brush with soy milk.

4 Bake in a preheated oven, 400°F/ 200°C, for 30–40 minutes, until golden brown. Serve immediately.

241

roasted bell pepper bread

serves four

1 tbsp vegan margarine,
    for greasing
1 red bell pepper, cut in half
    and seeded
1 yellow bell pepper, cut in half
    and seeded
2 fresh rosemary sprigs .
1 tbsp olive oil
¼ oz/10 g active dry yeast
1 tsp granulated sugar
1¼ cups lukewarm water
1 lb/450 g strong white bread flour
1 tsp salt

1 Grease a 9-inch/23-cm deep circular cake pan with margarine.

2 Place the bell pepper halves and rosemary sprigs in a shallow roasting pan. Pour over the oil and roast in a preheated oven, 400°F/200°C, for 20 minutes, or until slightly charred. Leave the peppers to cool slightly, then remove the skin, and cut the flesh into slices.

3 Place the yeast and sugar in a bowl and mix with ½ cup of the water. Let stand in a warm place for about 15 minutes, or until frothy.

4 Strain the flour and salt together into a large bowl. Stir in the yeast mixture and the remaining water and bring together with your fingers to form a smooth dough.

5 Knead the dough for 5 minutes, until smooth. Cover with oiled plastic wrap and let rise for about 30 minutes, or until doubled in size.

6 Cut the dough into 3 equal portions. Roll the portions into circles slightly larger than the cake pan.

7 Place 1 circle in the base of the pan so that it reaches up the sides by about ¾ inch/2 cm. Top with half of the bell pepper mixture. Strip the leaves from the rosemary sprigs and sprinkle half of them over the top.

8 Place the second circle of dough on top, followed by the remaining bell pepper mixture and rosemary leaves. Place the last circle of dough on top, pushing the edges of the dough down the sides of the pan.

9 Cover with oiled plastic wrap and let rise for 30–40 minutes. Bake for 45 minutes in the preheated oven, until golden. When the loaf is cooked it should sound hollow when tapped. Turn out onto a wire rack to cool slightly, then cut into slices to serve.

garlic & sage bread

serves six

1 tbsp vegan margarine,
  for greasing
2¼ cups brown bread flour
1 envelope active dry yeast
3 tbsp chopped fresh sage
2 tsp sea salt
3 garlic cloves, chopped finely
1 tsp honey
⅔ cup lukewarm water

1 Grease a cookie sheet with vegan margarine. Strain the flour into a large mixing bowl and add any bran remaining in the strainer.

2 Stir in the dry yeast, sage, and half of the sea salt. Reserve 1 teaspoon of the chopped garlic for sprinkling and stir the rest into the bowl. Add the honey and water and bring together to form a dough.

3 Turn the dough out onto a lightly floured counter and knead it for about 5 minutes. Alternatively, use an electric mixer with a dough hook.

4 Place the dough in a greased bowl, cover, and let rise in a warm place until doubled in size.

5 Knead the dough again for a few minutes to punch it down, then make it into a donut shape (see Cook's Tip), and place on the cookie sheet.

6 Cover and let rise for a further 30 minutes, or until springy to the touch. Sprinkle with the rest of the sea salt and garlic.

7 Bake the herb bread in a preheated oven, 400°F/200°C, for 25–30 minutes. Transfer to a wire rack to cool before slicing and serving.

COOK'S TIP
Roll the dough into a long sausage and then curve it into a donut shape. You can omit the sea salt for sprinkling, if you like.

sun-dried tomato loaf

serves four

¼ oz/10 g active dry yeast

1 tsp granulated sugar

1¼ cups lukewarm water

1 lb/450 g strong white bread flour,
  plus extra for dusting

1 tsp salt

2 tsp dried basil

2 tbsp sun-dried tomato paste or
  ordinary tomato paste

1 tbsp vegan margarine,
  for greasing

12 sun-dried tomatoes in oil,
  drained and cut into strips

1 Place the yeast and sugar in a small bowl and mix with ½ cup of the water. Let stand in a warm place for about 15 minutes, or until frothy.

2 Strain the flour and salt into a large mixing bowl. Make a well in the center and add the dried basil, yeast mixture, tomato paste, and half of the remaining water. Draw the flour into the liquid with a wooden spoon and bring together with your fingers to form a dough, adding the rest of the water gradually.

3 Turn the dough out onto a floured counter and knead for 5 minutes. Cover with oiled plastic wrap and let stand in a warm place for 30 minutes, or until doubled in size.

4 Lightly grease a 2-lb/900-g loaf pan with the vegan margarine.

5 Turn the dough out and knead in the sun-dried tomatoes. Knead for 2–3 minutes more.

6 Place the dough in the prepared pan. Let rise for 30–40 minutes, or until it has doubled in size again. Bake in a preheated oven, 375°F/ 190°C, for 30–35 minutes, or until golden. When the loaf is cooked, it should sound hollow when tapped on the base. Cool slightly on a wire rack and serve.

eggless sponge cake

serves eight

1 tbsp vegan margarine,
    for greasing
1¾ cups whole-wheat flour
4 tsp baking powder
¾ cup superfine sugar
6 tbsp sunflower oil
1 cup water
1 tsp vanilla extract
4 tbsp strawberry or raspberry
    reduced-sugar spread
superfine sugar,
    for dusting

COOK'S TIP

Standard margarine—packets
that are not labelled vegan—
may contain some animal
products, such as whey, butter
fat, or skim milk.

1 Grease 2 circular layer pans,
8-inches/20-cm wide, and line
them with baking parchment.

2 Strain the flour and baking
powder into a large bowl and
add any bran remaining in the strainer.
Stir in the sugar.

3 Pour in the oil, water, and vanilla
extract. Stir with a wooden spoon
for about 1 minute, until the mixture is
smooth, then divide among the
prepared pans.

4 Bake in a preheated oven, 350°F/
180°C, for 25–30 minutes, until
firm to the touch.

5 Let the sponge cakes cool in the
pans, then turn out, and transfer
to a wire rack to cool completely.
Remove the baking parchment.

VARIATION

To make a chocolate-flavored
sponge cake, replace
2 tablespoons of the whole-
wheat flour with unsweetened
cocoa. To make a citrus-flavored
sponge cake, add the grated rind
of ½ lemon or orange to the flour
in step 2. To make a coffee-
flavored sponge cake, replace
2 teaspoons of the flour with
instant coffee powder.

6 Place one sponge cake on a
serving plate. Cover with the
reduced-sugar fruit spread, spreading it
out to the edges, and place the other
sponge cake lightly on top.

7 Dust the eggless sponge cake
with a little superfine sugar
before serving.

baked cheesecake

serves six

4 tbsp vegan margarine, melted,
　　plus extra for greasing

2¼ cups graham cracker crumbs

⅓ cup chopped pitted dates

4 tbsp lemon juice

grated rind of 1 lemon

3 tbsp water

12 oz/350 g firm bean curd

⅔ cup apple juice

1 banana, mashed

1 tsp vanilla extract

1 mango, peeled, pitted,
　　and chopped

1 Lightly grease a 7-inch/18-cm circular loose-based cake pan with a little margarine.

2 Mix together the graham cracker crumbs and melted margarine in a bowl. Press the mixture into the base of the prepared pan.

3 Put the dates, lemon juice, lemon rind, and water into a pan and bring to a boil. Simmer for 5 minutes, until the dates are soft, then mash the mixture coarsely with a fork.

4 Place the mixture in a food processor with the bean curd, apple juice, mashed banana, and vanilla extract and process until the mixture forms a thick, smooth paste.

5 Pour the bean curd paste onto the prepared cracker-crumb base and level the surface with a spatula.

6 Bake in a preheated oven, 350°F/180°C, for 30–40 minutes, until lightly golden. Let cool in the pan, then chill thoroughly in the refrigerator before serving.

7 Place the chopped mango in a food processor and process until smooth. Serve the fruit purée as a sauce with the cheesecake.

pineapple upside-down cake

serves eight

¼ cup vegan margarine, diced, plus
extra for greasing

15 oz/425 g canned unsweetened
pineapple pieces in fruit
juice, drained, with the
juice reserved

4 tsp cornstarch

¼ cup brown sugar

½ cup water

grated rind of 1 lemon

SPONGE

4 tbsp sunflower oil

⅓ cup brown sugar

⅔ cup water

1¼ cups all-purpose flour

2 tsp baking powder

1 tsp ground cinnamon

1 Grease a deep 7-inch/18-cm circular cake pan with margarine. Mix the juice from the pineapple with the cornstarch to make a smooth paste. Put the paste in a pan with the sugar, margarine, and water, and stir over low heat until the sugar has dissolved. Bring to a boil and simmer for 2–3 minutes, until thickened. Let the pineapple syrup cool slightly.

2 To make the sponge, heat the oil, sugar, and water in a pan over low heat until the sugar has dissolved, but do not let it boil. Remove from the heat and let cool. Sift the flour, baking powder, and ground cinnamon into a mixing bowl. Pour in the cooled oil and sugar mixture and beat well to form a batter.

3 Place the pineapple pieces and lemon rind in the prepared pan. Pour over 4 tablespoons of pineapple syrup. Spoon the batter on top.

4 Bake in a preheated oven, 350°F/ 180°C, for 35–40 minutes, until set and a fine metal skewer inserted into the center comes out clean. Place a plate over the top and carefully invert, let stand for 5 minutes, then remove the pan. Serve immediately with the remaining syrup.

249

apricot slices

makes twelve

DOUGH

⅓ cup vegan margarine, diced, plus
    extra for greasing

1¾ cups whole-wheat flour

½ cup finely ground
    mixed nuts

4 tbsp water

soy milk, to glaze

FILLING

1 cup dried apricots

grated rind of 1 orange

1¼ cups apple juice

1 tsp ground cinnamon

⅓ cup raisins

COOK'S TIP

These slices will keep in an
airtight container for 3–4 days.

---

1 Lightly grease a 9-inch/23-cm
square cake pan. To make the
dough, place the flour and nuts in a
mixing bowl and rub in the margarine
with your fingertips until the mixture
resembles bread crumbs. Stir in the
water and bring together to form a
dough. Wrap in plastic wrap and chill
in the refrigerator for 30 minutes.

2 To make the filling, place the
apricots, orange rind, and apple
juice in a pan and bring to a boil.
Simmer gently for 30 minutes, until the
apricots are mushy. Cool slightly, then
place in a food processor and process
into a purée. Alternatively, press the
mixture through a fine strainer with the
back of a spoon. Add the cinnamon
and raisins and stir.

3 Remove the dough from the
refrigerator. Divide in half, roll out
one half, and use it to line the base of
the prepared pan. Spread the apricot
purée over the top, leaving a border
around the edges, and brush the edges
with water. Roll out the rest of the
dough to fit over the top. Place over
the purée and press the edges to seal.

4 Prick the top of the dough with
a fork and brush with soy milk.
Bake in a preheated oven, 400°F/
200°C, for 20–25 minutes, until
golden. Let cool slightly before cutting
into 12 bars. Serve the apricot slices
warm or cold.

date & apricot tart

serves eight

1¾ cups all-purpose whole-wheat
   flour, plus extra for dusting
½ cup ground mixed nuts
⅓ cup vegan margarine, diced
4 tbsp water
1 cup chopped dried apricots
1⅓ cups chopped pitted dates
scant 2 cups apple juice
1 tsp ground cinnamon
grated rind of 1 lemon
soy custard, to serve (optional)

1 Place the flour and ground nuts in a mixing bowl and rub in the margarine with your fingertips until the mixture resembles bread crumbs. Stir in the water and bring together to form a dough. Wrap in plastic wrap and chill in the refrigerator for 30 minutes.

2 Meanwhile, place the apricots and dates in a pan with the apple juice, cinnamon, and lemon rind. Bring to a boil, cover, and simmer over low heat for about 15 minutes, until the fruit has softened. Mash the fruit into a purée and set aside.

3 Remove the dough from the refrigerator. Reserve a small ball of dough for making lattice strips. Roll out the rest of the dough into a circle on a lightly floured counter and use it to line a 9-inch/23-cm loose-based tart pan.

4 Spread the fruit purée evenly over the base of the tart shell. Roll out the reserved dough and cut into strips ½ inch/1 cm wide. Cut the strips to fit the tart and twist them across the top of the fruit to form a decorative lattice

pattern. Moisten the edges of the dough strips with a little water and press the ends firmly against the rim of the tart to seal.

5 Bake in a preheated oven, 400°F/200°C, for 25–30 minutes, until golden brown. Cut into the tart into slices and serve immediately with soy custard, if you like.

fruit crumble

serves six

1 tbsp vegan margarine,
　for greasing
6 pears, peeled
1 tbsp chopped preserved ginger
1 tbsp dark brown sugar
2 tbsp orange juice
CRUMBLE TOPPING
1½ cups all-purpose flour
6 tbsp vegan margarine, diced
¼ cup sliced almonds
⅓ cup rolled oats
1¾ oz/50 g dark brown sugar
soy custard, to serve (optional)

VARIATION

Stir 1 teaspoon ground
allspice into the crumble
mixture in step 3 for added
flavor, if you like.

---

1 Lightly grease a 4-cup/1-litre ovenproof dish with the vegan margarine.

2 Core the pears, cut them into fourths, and slice them. Place the pear slices in a bowl with the ginger, sugar, and orange juice and stir to blend. Spoon the mixture evenly across the base of the prepared dish.

3 To make the crumble topping, strain the flour into a large mixing bowl. Add the margarine and rub it in with your fingertips until the mixture resembles fine bread crumbs. Add the sliced almonds, then the rolled oats and sugar. Mix together until thoroughly blended.

4 Sprinkle the crumble topping evenly over the pear and ginger mixture in the dish, pressing it down gently with the back of a spoon.

5 Bake in a preheated oven, 375°F/ 190°C, for 30 minutes, until the topping is golden and the fruit tender. Serve the crumble immediately with soy custard, if you like.